A Light in the Shadows

A Light in the Shadows

Emerging From the
Darkness of Depression

Personal Reflections of a Counselor

William L. Coleman

SERVANT PUBLICATIONS
ANN ARBOR, MICHIGAN

Vine Books is an imprint of Servant Publications especially designed to serve
evangelical Christians.

All Scripture quotations, unless indicated, are taken from the HOLY BIBLE,
NEW INTERNATIONAL VERSION. © 1973, 1978, 1984 by International
Bible Society. Used by permission of Zondervan Publishing House. All rights
reserved.

Published by Servant Publications
P.O. Box 8617
Ann Arbor, Michigan 48107

Cover design: Eric Walljasper

00 01 02   03   10 9 8 7 6 5 4 3 2 1

Printed in the United States of America
ISBN 1-56955-151-0

Cataloging-In-Publication Data on file at the Library of Congress.

Contents

For Those Who Understand

This book is written for those who know that real depression is different from pouting because your lottery number didn't come through or sulking when the Yankees lose. Depression hangs around like a dark cloud, stealing your energy and sapping your will to move on.

Fortunately, great strides have been taken toward helping those who suffer from this affliction. Many are now better able to work through depression and to learn skills that can hold this monster at bay. A decade or two ago, too many of us believed we could not be helped.

This is not an ABC book on how to defeat depression. Rather, it is a book of "connecting," written by someone who has been there, many times over. I've seen the bottom of the pit and the peak of the mountain; I've traveled every foot of the path between the two.

In this book I discuss how I learned to cope with depression. I talk about what has not worked for me—and I share what has. I talk about what faith has done for me, as well as what it has not. For most of us depression is a journey. The journey never quite ends, but there can be great periods of good health along the way.

Since the first section is based on my own experience, it won't match that of everyone else. My prayer is that my story will be familiar enough to encourage those who travel through its pages.

If I had my way, people would read this book and then see a good therapist. My dream won't come true every time, but I am content that sometimes it will.

I want to express my sincere gratitude to Heidi Hess Saxton, editor at Servant Publications. Her enthusiasm for the project and persistence in seeing it through have been outstanding.

As a counselor in private practice, I see many who are struggling with depression. I have been painstakingly careful not to use the stories of my clients.

Have a good read. It isn't all cheerful, but neither is it merely a ride through the tunnel. May your life be enriched and strengthened.

Bill Coleman
July 1, 1999

It is remarkable how much consolation and hope we can receive from authors....

Their courage to enter so deeply into human suffering and to become present to their own pain gave them the power to speak healing words.

Henri J.M. Nouwen

PART ONE

My Journey in the Shadows

The Parent Trap

When a child is neglected or abused by a parent, the mental anguish is almost maddening. As a child I knew I was not being cared for. I had few clothes, and the ones I had were not clean. The house was so messy that I never invited anyone over. Meals were often not made. A man lived in our house in a bedroom with my mother; my father lived alone in a back room.

My mother and father were seldom home. I was regularly given a small amount of money so I could attend a movie and stay away. I could not trust my mother because she might be drinking, and her word was almost always undependable.

What I knew about parents, based on my own, never jelled with what I heard and saw in other parents. The word "mother" failed to conjure up the same loving image it seemed to suggest for others.

My mind and heart were trapped. The image that should have been did not match the reality, and I could not figure out why. The mental pressure became mental torture as I tried to reconcile my life with the lives of others.

Words are too weak to describe the agony I felt because I couldn't trust a parent. Only those who have suffered in this trap can appreciate its terror. Those who read and theorize about it will never feel the anxiety, the emptiness, or the horror. Life made no sense to me, and yet I was expected to forge ahead into a threatening world without even the most basic emotional support.

Imagine a jungle thick with undergrowth, trees, and vines. At any second a viper, jaguar, or deadly spider could strike. Each step could collapse into a hole. Torrential rains might start at any time. Terrible heat saps your energy. Who can say what danger or challenge awaits around the next tree? Then try to picture a six-year-old wandering alone through that bewildering maze.

I was tempted to protest: "Why aren't my parents here to take care of me? This isn't fair. Parents are supposed to be fair and caring. My mind can't sift all of this out." I crossed my arms over my eyes because I couldn't handle life as I saw it.

Brown Tennis Shoes

Ted's family was the only one in our neighborhood that was poorer than ours. His family lived beside an alley. Whenever people made jokes about poor people, I knew they were talking about Ted and not about me. I'm embarrassed now that I looked down on him.

That fact gave a bit of comfort, but it didn't really improve my condition.

The city condemned the house we rented and placed a huge sign over the front porch. That sign made me feel different.

My family bought me combat boots because they would last. In those days combat boots made me feel different.

My family put our name in to receive holiday food delivered by students.

You get the picture.

Nothing in school went particularly well. I was hostile in junior high and got into many fights. I flunked a lot of subjects but got pushed along anyway. For a few weeks they took me out of regular class and put me in the "ungraded." There I met students who were more rebellious than I and a teacher who was worse than all of us. I liked it there. I actually grieved when they put me back in regular class.

Everything was going steadily downhill, until one day I entered a track meet at the Virginia Avenue playground near my house. It was a long day and I took first place in two or three events and did well in a couple more.

That was the day I began to dream. I saw my ticket out. High school was going to be different. I didn't have to be a loser all my life. The girls would notice. The coaches would pat me on the back. I could develop one of those athletic struts when I walked down the corridor.

Excitedly I took the message to my dad. Sometimes he did the best he could, and this time he listened carefully. He liked the idea and smiled.

All I needed, I explained, was a new pair of tennis shoes. With new shoes I could run even faster and people would notice how really gifted I was. And to myself I thought, "They will like me."

My dad was pleased and he promised to get me a pair of new shoes to start my high school career. Not right away, but eventually my father took me to a store to buy those anxiously awaited shoes.

I didn't need anything fancy. We didn't have stylish athletic shoes in those days anyway. I just needed average, so I could be like everybody else.

We hadn't been in the store long before my father turned to a pair of shoes and announced that this was what he could afford. They were the cheapest, drabbest brown pair of tennis shoes in the entire world. Both shoes seemed to have "poor, loser, worthless" written all over them.

Without protest I thanked my father for the shoes. Walking home I knew my world was over. There was no way up. No way out. No bright tomorrow.

After pondering this terrible disappointment, I decided to take action. Removing a bottle of iodine from the medicine cabinet, I drank all eight ounces. I sat down and waited to die. Not knowing much about prayer, I began to repeat the Lord's

13

Prayer, anxiously anticipating my own death.

A few minutes later I went downstairs and told my father what I had done. I can still see the look on his face. Because we had no car, my father and I walked to the nearby Fifth Precinct Police Station.

The tennis shoes hadn't done it. Neither had my father. Fifteen years of feeling left out, second-rate, and useless had loaded the gun. By now it had a hair trigger, waiting for the slightest jar to set it off. If it hadn't been the shoes, some other event was bound to have put this tragic attempt in motion. Something had to give.

The Proverbial Straw

E very so often the newspaper carries a horrifying headline such as "High-School Teen Dies of Self-Inflicted Gunshot Wound" or "Girl Killed in Car Accident." Reading further, you discover that the football captain shot himself after losing the homecoming game, or the girl jumped in front of a car after having a fight with her mother.

At first glance, these stories don't make much sense. Why would someone commit suicide over a lost game or a simple argument? And yet, if someone were to dig deeper, perform a kind of "psychological autopsy," he or she might uncover some of the many underlying reasons that caused the bomb to go off.

After drinking eight ounces of iodine, I spent nine days in a Washington, D.C., hospital, "under observation." Every day I spent a few minutes talking to a doctor who spoke broken English. It didn't bother me, except that I hoped he understood my answers a lot better than I understood his questions.

From there I was released to a caring doctor who asked wonderful questions; but he soon passed me on to a social worker, who session after session merely asked, "How do you feel?" Finally I said I felt like I was not coming back. Then I left. That, too, was unfortunate, because I did need help. I wish I had connected with a good counselor of some kind.

From that low point I did rise up, to a large extent because of my conversion experience. Like Paul on the road to

Damascus, I, too, had a dramatic crisis encounter with my faith in Christ.

My conversion half healed me. But, believe me, at the time, half-healing was very important.

Consequently I moved up into a half-depressed state. Some days I was highly functional. Other days I crawled along the baseboards of life like a water bug. There was more work to be done, and I failed to take care of it.

The worst part of being a survivor of an aborted suicide was that I believed I was still "a suicide waiting to happen". Eventually, at some unmarked place, under some unidentified circumstances, I fully expected to end my own life. The idea of living to thirty years of age often seemed a remote possibility at best. Even after I had a wife and three children I kept open the option of bailing out of this life if I chose.

It was like I had a sign hanging in the back of my brain that read, "Someday you will end it." I never touched the sign. Something told me that the sign was right. Life really was that unbearable at times.

Today I know I could have found someone to help me get rid of the sign in my brain. The cloud could have been pushed back, possibly even dissipated altogether. I did not have to live under the shadow of suicide as long as I did.

I call as my heart grows faint;
lead me to the rock that is higher than I.

PSALM 61:2b

16

God Sent a Nurse

God works in mysterious ways. If we could explain those ways they would no longer be a mystery, so there is little sense in trying. This much is certain in my life: First there was A, second came B, and then C came roaring in. Why they happened I am uncertain, but I know they did.

(A) I was admitted to the Washington, D.C., General Hospital for mental observation.

(B) There I met a nurse who was a Christian.

(C) I later attended the church where she was a member and invited Christ into my life.

Exactly how, or even why, those events became connected I cannot say. I know only that I am eternally thankful for the results.

As a teen placed under mental observation, I found it to be a bewildering experience. Living in a ward where a wide range of characters were kept for a wide range of reasons was more than I could absorb. Not unlike the book *One Flew Over the Cuckoo's Nest,* individuals were there for running naked through the snow, for pulling knives on family members, and for hearing voices. They were no better than me, no worse than me, and we made up an odd assortment of society.

Most of the time I was not frightened. My state of mind was closer to despair. However, when a large, muscular man shouted loudly that I should shut up, I distinctly remember shutting up.

The staff, I thought, would have made an interesting study. Several appeared in need of treatment themselves, more patients than employees. Yet for the most part the staff was professional and businesslike, though not particularly compassionate.

There were a few notable exceptions, of course. I recall one kindly, white-haired man, dressed in khaki pants and shirt. His voice was calm and pleasant. He would have made a terrific uncle.

And then there was that nurse. She was an angel. Young, attractive, and kind, her spirit reached out and touched others. She could be firm when she needed to be. I can remember playing with a pencil and pretending to stab myself in the temple. After three or four mock motions, she very firmly took it away. I saw it as a sign that she cared.

One day the pretty nurse told me, "I don't know what the future holds for you, but I do know you don't belong in here."

What a rush. Someone believed in me. That's all she said.

On another day the same nurse asked me where I lived, and I told her. "Oh," she said, "I go to church only a few blocks from there. Come visit sometime."

Those words stuck. It was the same church I had attended for about a year as a child. I wanted to go back there.

The first Sunday I showed up, I listened to every word in the sermon and I asked Christ into my life. Somehow the A, B, and C connected. Not long afterward I attended the nurse's wedding in that same church. As I sat by the aisle, she and her husband walked past me during the recessional, and with one quick glance she looked my way and simply said, "Hi, Bill."

There is no way to explain it. I simply know it's true. Some nurses really are angels.

*For he will command his angels concerning you
to guard you in all your ways.*

PSALM 91:11

How the Spiritual Helps

I didn't grow up in church. No one taught me the old hymns or when to stand up or why an usher was supposed to help me find a seat.

But there were some things I discovered fairly quickly once I became a Christian. When Christ came into my life, I found out what it meant to have real "joy." I had a new group of friends who surrounded me, and I became active in ways I had never dreamed. That part of my spiritual life was like a new jacket and shoes. I was extremely grateful for my new Christian life.

Unfortunately, when I became a Christian I also assumed that believers did not get depressed. They were expected to smile, serve, get excited, and roll along. I don't know who taught me this, I suppose no one in particular, but that was clearly the impression I had.

Consequently, I came to believe that my continual struggle with depression was weird. Somehow I felt I was flunking the Christian life because I frequently sank to the bottom of the emotional ocean.

I wish someone in a group, from a pulpit, in a class, or even in a private discussion had simply said, "Sometimes believers go in the dumper, too." What a big help that would have been.

I was one of those believers who wasn't well disciplined, and often I felt guilty about it. The guilt often triggered depression. Unfortunately, this misconception in my newfound faith often added to my dark side.

Now I know that Job, Elijah, and Jonah are just a few of the biblical characters who also wrestled with depression. I wish that I had known that then. See for yourself:

[And Job said,] "May the day of my birth perish,
and the night it was said, 'A boy is born!'"

JOB 3:3

[Elijah] came to a broom tree, sat down under it and prayed
that he might die. "I have had enough, Lord," he said. "Take
my life; I am no better than my ancestors."

1 KINGS 19:4

But Jonah was greatly displeased and became angry ... "Now,
O Lord, take away my life, for it is better for me to die than to
live."

JONAH 4:1, 3

It is all right to get down—really down. These men did ... and they still had a vibrant faith in the heavenly Father.

A spiritual life can definitely help with our struggle over depression. But faith is sometimes not enough by itself. There are times when therapy, medication, and other approaches can join hands with the spiritual and help us deal with the vagaries of our moods.

Doubtless some have had a conversion experience or a renewal and have never been depressed since. But many others have reached out to a spiritual life and to therapy at the same time, and have found tremendous help.

Someone Who Cared

It wasn't easy, growing up. I was failing school; without social hope; at war with teachers and administration alike. I floundered, waiting for the total wreck which was almost certain to come.

Every now and again during my childhood the cloud lifted, if only briefly. No one actually intervened. No one lifted me from my surroundings or substantially altered my course. Yet every so often I met someone who seemed to sense what I faced, someone who cared—at least for a little while. Still, in the natural order of events I struggled.

Then I heard about someone who cared who would stay with me and never leave. That someone was Jesus. Old-fashioned, churchgoing, repent-or-perish Jesus. And it clicked. He became my life preserver on the raging sea. He gave me purpose. He gave me acceptance. He even gave me forgiveness for all the shame and inadequacy I was carrying.

For the first time I had something that resembled a rock—immovable, dependable, solid, and eternal. Day in and day out, I now had a friend who cared—and who wouldn't leave me alone. My crude, shapeless life began to take form. I had needed a reason to live, and Jesus handed it to me.

I had been found. I understood that. What I didn't understand was that the child inside was still lost.

On the outside I had begun to take form, but the child inside continued to weep. At times I felt bewildered and sad.

And so I became a man who roared. I took on the battles of the day, winning some and losing others. Yet, inside, the trapped child longed to be loved. Locked away, he knew nothing of the freedom so often enjoyed by my adult self.

When I discovered how much God cared for me, I knew that I could make it. I also knew that if the adult in me could make it, then ultimately there was also hope for the child. From that rock anything was possible.

It was as if a long rope were tied around my waist and the other end lashed tightly to that rock of faith. The storms did not cease, though they came less often and usually with milder winds. They still roared across me every now and then.

But, thankfully, the rope held and the rock did not move. Without that rock I might have been washed out to sea long ago.

Save me, O God, for the waters have come up to my neck.
I sink in the miry depths, where there is no foothold.
I have come into the deep waters; the floods engulf me.
I am worn out calling for help; my throat is parched.
My eyes fail, looking for my God.

PSALM 69:1-3

Where Did My Childhood Go?

At its best, childhood should be a garden where children play, explore, and develop in relative ease and happiness. Every child should have the privilege of security, love, and peace. It is too bad that so many of us were attacked, abused, or neglected in the garden.

The loss of childhood has a lasting effect on millions of us. When we reach adulthood our wounds and deprivation leave us not quite ready to tackle the next stage of life. At the age of thirty or much more we are still asking whether anyone loves us—asking whether we are safe anywhere or with anyone.

Pity the poor people who marry us. Our spouses will always be trying to do more or say more to make up for the great holes left from our youth.

Those who were abused or neglected may have to rebuild themselves from the inside out. Some are able to accomplish this alone. Others do it with a significant other. A few find a counselor they can trust.

No one owes us anything, except our parents. The fact that they conceived us, either by accident or by design, marks the obligation to meet our basic needs. If they can't, they must find someone else who can. Neglect is never an option.

The worst losses of childhood are the ones we can't explain. War, famine, natural disasters, even illness are things we can deal with. But how can any of us say our parents had a choice and yet chose not to care for us? The very possibility defies our ability to comprehend or decipher.

Fortunate is the adult who one day recognizes what he or she has lost. As miserable as it is, this is at least a beginning. The first step to a healthier mind is to understand what is missing.

Not every depressed person lost his or her childhood. Some had caring parents. Yet many of us can trace the sources of our pain to those empty years.

The road to recovery is not filled with ice-cream cones and roller-coaster rides. These cannot restore our childhoods.

More importantly, we must come to appreciate ourselves for the lovable people we are, and always were. It is too bad the right people weren't there to love us in our childhood.

Why We Sing Country Blues

Those who aren't attracted to sad songs have trouble understanding people who are. Why would anyone want to listen to slow music and depressing lyrics?

Why do I like to hear about loss? I enjoy a sincere country tune about a person who lost his wife, his girlfriend, his health, or even his truck. Give me a song filled with pathos and despair. Whether it's Hank Williams (who blended country and blues) or George Jones, Merle Haggard or Garth Brooks, they each have identified with pain. Their songs put a lump in my throat and a tear in my eye.

After listening to country blues for decades, the answer finally came to me. I like to hear other people sing about grief because it helps me to mourn my own childhood.

My childhood was lost due to unnatural causes. To this day, I don't understand why it happened. Was I simply not bright enough or cute enough or special enough? Why was the child in me so neglected that he was lost altogether?

I've had to mourn for that lost child. So all my life I have listened to all kinds of singers express their grief. The musicians lost their parents, their homes, their children, their dreams. Listening to them mourn helps me. How do they express their loss? How do they cry? How do they say goodbye? How do they pull themselves together and move on?

There is a reason for sad songs. They connect with sad

people, even when the sadness is over different themes. After all, grief is grief.

For that reason, I have trouble identifying with most church music. Seldom does it reach inside and speak to my loss. The exception is the psalms. The psalmist sang about loss, agony, fear, and confusion. He wrestled with God in his lyrics. I connect with that.

You don't have to be ignorant or tone deaf to enjoy country blues. Sometimes all you need is an aching desire to mourn.

> *O Lord, do not rebuke me in your anger*
> *or discipline me in your wrath.*
> *Be merciful to me, Lord, for I am faint;*
> *O Lord, heal me, for my bones are in agony.*
> *My soul is in anguish.*
> *How long, O Lord, how long?*
>
> PSALM 6:1-3

Deciding to Be Myself

Finding one's identity is easy for some, but terribly hard for others. It takes great courage to be yourself when you feel alone.

Growing up in a family full of secrets, I had little sense of who I was or how I "fit" into the total lay of life. I had no bearings, no sense of belonging. I was lost in the woods.

At first I tried to uncover my identity by comparing myself with others. I would look at one person. "Am I funny like him?"

Thinking this over, I would scan the room for the next one. "Am I as smart as she is?"

"Am I 'Mr. Personality'?"

"Am I 'Mr. Nice Guy'?"

It was an exercise in futility, of course. I never discovered who I was this way. I stayed lost in that great, dark woods. Neither the trees nor the stars, the rocks nor the moss gave me a clue as to where I was.

In a sense I did not exist. Inside my head and heart there was no one home. In the end I discovered that no one would ever be able to lead me out of the forest. I had to get my own bearings. I had to make my own path. Sing my own song in the night. Whisper words of courage to my own trembling heart.

Unable to be like others, I was forced to become myself. Not better than others; better or worse was not the issue. Finding a way to continue my journey through the forest was all that mattered. I had to be myself to survive.

I found that this process of self-discovery was not without cost. Creating my own bearings, I messed up a great deal. Sometimes it meant that I hurt people I never wished to hurt. Sometimes I ached with loneliness. Yet I was never again totally lost.

When I see young people today, ax in one hand, machete in the other, hacking their own paths through life, my heart jumps for joy.

Make your own way, I want to tell them. *There is no path like yours.*

My Love Affair With Depression

The saying goes something like this: If you are placed in a cage with a five-hundred-pound gorilla, you have two choices. Either fight the gorilla or make friends with it.

One way to survive depression is to make friends with it. Part of my experience with the dark side is that I made depression my "mistress." I came to appreciate its beautiful side, complete with charms, comforts, and safety. Unsure how life would treat me, I could count on my deeper mood and I knew how it would react. Up to a point.

A date with depression was an evening or two of gentle acceptance. If I would forsake all else for a few hours, to brood alone, my mistress would woo and welcome me with open arms. But I had to come alone. I had to disconnect from hope and sink quietly into the depths of despair.

That's all that was asked. My date held no high excitement. It did not try to motivate or discuss future goals. Give up, sit still, think in circles, spiral downwardly—that was her message for me.

Whether our meeting was a date for a day or rendezvous for a week, she was pleased either way. No questions. No nagging. No embarrassing remarks. Only total acceptance. As long as I left everything else, everyone else, outside the door.

Most of us eventually become disenchanted with the old girl. Then we move on to periods of happiness or a form of cure. But the fact is, few of us ever throw her phone number away. We never know when we might want to give her a call, just for old times' sake.

Some friends, small groups, and counselors act horrified when they hear about depression in the role of mistress. They envision an ugly, mean whore who leaves everyone repulsed and causes them to scream and run. But some of us know better.

Drug addicts often describe their experiences as destructive and disabling. They speak of pain, torture, and loss of control. Yet in the next breath a twinkle appears in their eyes as they wistfully imagine that someday they might be able to date the cruel damsel again.

Those with the most appreciation for the dark angel of depression must admit she is both enjoyable and evil. Closing one eye to the evil, we want to hunt her up again for the pleasure she has to offer.

This is one complicated and mysterious mistress.

Whose Fault Is It, Anyway?

For you have been my hope, O Sovereign Lord,
my confidence since my youth.
From birth I have relied on you;
you brought me forth from my mother's womb.
PSALM 71:5-6

How much comfort would it be if I blamed my depression on my parents? It would be easy enough. They made mistakes. More than that, they even did some evil things. Parents are easy scapegoats; and I could find counselors who would agree that my background contributed a lot to my pain.

Yet even if I identify someone else as the source of my troubles, I still have my troubles. This is because my troubles are mine.

How I handle my troubles today is my responsibility. I cannot expect my parents to mount horses and ride to my rescue. I'm an adult. I must deal with my own problems.

It would be easy to crawl through life as a sad, pitiful victim. "Look at poor me. I had parent problems." We are victims if we choose to be. But would that be fun?

There is value in understanding how my parents and others have contributed to my depression. That may help to clear up the picture. It is quite another thing to expect my parents to heal me. I must take charge of my own healing process, and if necessary find the means to make it happen.

31

If I step on a skate and fall, certainly the person who left the skate on the path must share the blame for my sprained ankle. But it helps no one if I sit on the ground and pout because that person does not take me to the doctor.

The sprained ankle is partly that other person's fault. Healing is totally my responsibility.

There is no doubt that childhood experiences contributed enormously to my depression, and once in a while I feel very sorry for myself. But then I look in the mirror and tell myself, as honestly as possible, that healing is my responsibility. I alone can really do something about it.

It's Hard to Get Close to Others

The major theme of my first twenty years of life was a simple one: *No one will be permitted to know what I'm really like. No one will cross the secret threshold and enter into the metal vault where my heart is kept locked away.*

They must never know how I love or hate. They can never see what I fear or hope. Even my strengths and weaknesses must be guarded, lest some see who I really am and give an opinion.

I was like a porcupine with its quills out. Everything was secretive. No one could visit our house. No one must see the holes in my socks. No one was to meet my parents or ask any questions about our lives. Who told me to be so secretive? No one. That was simply how I chose to cope with my bewildering life.

It was a question of survival. My soul could not go on if it were exposed to the sunlight. Like Dracula, the real me moved about in darkness and fled quickly as dawn broke through the window pane.

After twenty years or so of this routine I became tired of hiding, but I wasn't sure what to do about it. If for twenty years you train yourself to wear disguises, masks, and phony noses, it's hard to break the habit. If for two decades you fight desperately to keep the real you tucked away, it's understandably difficult to one day pull open your robe and say, "Look, this is who I really am."

Difficult won't describe it. Frightening! Horrible! Terrifying!

Each is closer to the truth. And later, when a teacher, leader, or counselor tells you casually, "You know, you're going to have to open up," you shrink back and head for a hole, like a prairie dog running from a ferret.

But by the grace of God, someone may come along. Someone who loves you. At first you will hold that person at arm's length. Even if you marry him or her. And then slowly, painfully, inch by inch, you might crack open the vault and ever so slowly push the door ajar. Only then will that person begin to see the real you.

And if he or she stays long enough, and endures the unreasonable cold, and pays the awful price, that loving person will begin to see the intimate, heartfelt you. Complete with wounds, scars, and loving patches. And if it works, that person will be really glad he or she got to know the real you.

The person who stayed and paid to see the real you deserves all your love. We meet few heroes as we journey through this life, and this loved one is the greatest of them all.

Love and faithfulness meet together;
righteousness and peace kiss each other.
Faithfulness springs forth from the earth,
and righteousness looks down from heaven.
The Lord will indeed give what is good.

PSALM 85:10-12

Am I Crazy?

I think I really am. There was a time when I was afraid to admit that, but of late it rolls off the tongue a bit easier. What finally convinced me was the realization that all of us are crazy to some extent.

What a relief this is. Previously I tried desperately to keep my craziness hidden. The very word sent shivers up and down my spine. What if people discovered the awful truth and knew how nuts I really was? What would they do then?

There is no hiding it. I'm crazy. You're crazy. We are all a little loony. Sometimes I think a small problem is a huge catastrophe. Often I worry about the wrong things. Once in a while I have illusions of my own grandeur. Other days I call myself worthless.

I'm nuts just like you're nuts. We might as well admit it.

Am I mentally ill? Beyond a doubt I sometimes am. I become physically ill from time to time. I get the flu, a stiff back, headaches, and my elbows show some signs of arthritis.

Mentally, it's the same. Occasionally I believe people are out to get me. Sometimes I think the clerk at the local grocery store doesn't really like me. Once in a while I go to the office wondering if the people who come in are going to find out what I'm incapable of. I can get anxious over the slightest thing and feel my adrenaline pumping full-speed.

I have a little mental illness here and a little mental illness there. When I'm not feeling sharp I usually rise up and do something about it. Other times I simply let it ride, and then I get mentally sicker before I get mentally better.

Once I accepted my craziness, I found myself far easier to live with. At one period of my life I would get depressed about getting depressed. My logic was that I was too good ever to get depressed. My thinking was, "I feel lost, and I must be damaged if I feel lost." There was double evidence that I was defective. That's a very dangerous situation, and a difficult one from which to recover.

Finally, reality arrived. If I am crazy like everyone else, it's all right to get depressed. I'm nuts and that's human. I have a bit of mental illness. It's like a cold, and I need to do something about it.

Don't bother to argue, "I can't be mentally ill." Of course you can. What makes you so special? That's like saying you can't get a headache.

Depression is something that normal people get. As one song says, "We go half crazy now and then." Crazy isn't a technical term. It simply means that most of us get off balance. That's the human condition.

On my bed I remember you;
I think of you through the watches of the night.
Because you are my help, I sing in the shadow of your wings.
My soul clings to you; your right hand upholds me.

PSALM 63:6-8

Like a Fever

Depression is like a fever. Its presence suggests that an infection exists somewhere in my mind, soul, heart, or psyche. Depression is real. The cause of the depression must be dealt with just as we must find the cause of a fever.

For years I believed my problem was chronic depression which sometimes turned acute, a serious situation, to be sure. Any number of destructive things might have overwhelmed me during those episodes.

Today I tend to look at my occasional depression as a symptom and not as the problem itself. Since I have no reason to believe my depression has a physical origin, I must look at it as situational. Events happen to expose my own inadequacies and send me into the dumper.

Ultimately I do myself a disservice by merely dealing with the symptoms. Beneath the surface lies a cause or two, or maybe even a handful. If I could change these, ever so gently or ever so firmly, I might be able to regain my health.

The causes of my depression might not be physical, like a liver or a knee, but they are just as real: Grief. Broken heart. Loss. Discouragement. Displacement. Divorce. Hurt. They are as factual as any cyst or bunion ever was.

The challenge for me is to find the source of the fever. Sometimes I am fairly good at trolling for the causes. Other times I need to ask someone else to join me in the search. It's important that I find the right person, someone who will be wise enough to help and not to hurt.

If I merely tell myself, "I will not get depressed," quite often I end up depressed. But when I refocus and go after the symptoms, the depression usually lifts.

I go after the depression "fever symptoms" if they seem threatening. Once the fever is stabilized, I start writing down causes for the depression.

Naturally there is a day, now and then, when none of this works. Depression rolls over me, I lose my cool entirely, and there is no way I can calmly, logically look for reasons. On those days I have a tough tussle with the old monster.

Give us aid against the enemy,
for the help of man is worthless.

PSALM 60:11

Life in a Cave

When life is dark and there seems little hope of escaping the despair, it feels as if you are lost in a deep, dank cave.

Having lived in a mental cave for far too long, I decided it was time to find the light and make my way to the surface. It occurred to me that there were three ways to discover freedom.

First, I could keep searching on my own, without any aid from anyone. Walking in the damp dark, I used my own strength to climb through one channel and then the next. Occasionally I rose up higher and even drier and my condition improved. Sometimes I believed I saw the light, but eventually it would become lost as I turned the next corner.

A second way I tried to free myself from the cave was to follow someone else's light. A flashlight from on high sent its beam in my direction, and I followed it as far as I could. Usually this kind of light came from books, articles, or bits of advice picked up here and there. Sometimes the light was sparse and contradictory. But for a while it gave me more hope than despair.

On rare occasions the third kind of guidance came into the cave, found me, and helped take me to the surface. Normally this meant that someone made the extraordinary effort of getting involved in my life. This was not an easy task. Most of the time I chased help away and made myself difficult to find.

Experience has taught me that I should not have ignored

any of the three. I needed to thrust myself toward the mouth of the cave. As difficult and sometimes devastating as that was, I had to try. Likewise, I needed to pick up a bit of information here and glean some wisdom there. Thirdly, I wish I had stayed with a counselor in the early years and let him lead me by the hand toward the daylight.

Cave dwelling is better suited for bats. They know their way around and don't seem to mind hanging upside down. Spelunking may be all right for short visits by humans, but long stays are chilly and uncomfortable.

Hopefully each of us will eventually face up to the task of finding our way to daylight. Which way is it going to be? Will we search on our own, or seek guidance from books, or ask for help from a friend, support group, or counselor? And if our first attempt fails, will we have the courage to try another way?

Suicide Notes

I once read the farewell message of a college-age Christian girl. Her faith in the life hereafter had grown much larger than her faith in life here on earth.

She taught me a great deal about faith and suicide. From her I learned that one did not have to abandon faith in God in order to contemplate suicide. She looked forward to being absorbed into the grace of God. The young lady's logic had become disoriented, but I appreciated looking at her thought process.

A copy of a suicide note that I have kept was written by a sportswriter. The newspaper in a large Midwestern city published it on the sports page, in its entirety.

Briefly he wrote of the athletes he'd had the privilege of meeting, as well as the one or two he could have lived without. He fondly remembered playing ball with his children, and stressed how much he would miss them. Finally he bade good-bye to his beloved wife. His well-crafted letter was a piece of art. The fine writing itself seemed to indicate what a terrible waste his death was.

Years ago, I admired suicide notes. I admired them, that is, until I realized how twisted and distorted they really were. Today I recognize them as the final cry of a hurting life.

No longer do I consider these letters "art." There is too much personal pain and tragedy in them. My heart weeps over the irretrievable loss.

Never again will I pen suicide notes in my mind or fantasize funerals where people line up to say, "So long." Forget it. I'm going to outlive them all. Friends and acquaintances will not be around to give me a last salute.

At one time I admired these letters. They were decisive, a sign that someone, who may have wrestled for years over choosing life or death, had finally made a decision. At a time in my life when it was difficult to make any decision at all, this had impressed me.

But now I, too, have made a choice. I choose to live. I'll write my notes about life. I'll pen my poetry about the challenges that make me get up in the morning. And when it comes time for me to write the final page in my book of life, it will be full of words of gratitude. The Lord is giving me a whale of a ride.

Even when I am old and gray,
do not forsake me, O God,
till I declare your power to the next generation,
your might to all who are to come.

PSALM 71:18

Lies I Told Myself

I am in pain and distress;
may your salvation, O God, protect me.
PSALM 69:29

For a large part of my adult life I considered suicide a genuine option and actually assumed that it would be my final act. In order to rationalize this possibility I had to tell myself several lies, and repeat them over and over. It isn't easy keeping a lie alive in your imagination, but if you repeat it often enough, it sounds like truth. I don't know if other potential suicides lie to themselves, but I know that I did.

One of the big lies I told myself was that my children would be better off without me. Despite every fact to the contrary, I was somehow able to keep this balloon in the air.

The truth of the matter is that my children would have been devastated by my voluntary death. Financially, emotionally, psychologically, spiritually—on every front—their lives would have been shattered. Nothing worse could have happened to them. Every argument I made to myself to the contrary was feeble.

But at the time it all seemed like strong logic to me.

A second whopper I told myself was that I was so useless my death would stop me from messing up anything more. What I refused to accept was that it would also end any good that I would otherwise accomplish. My lying mind told me I could do no good.

We don't have to be Mother Teresa to see some of the ways we touch others. The lie of uselessness does terrible damage to our desire to live, and it certainly hurt mine.

A third lie was one of my favorites. This bit of tortured thinking suggested that my family would understand. They would love me and forgive me, like flower children dancing in the garden of life, celebrating what a great husband and dad they had had, who did the right thing by catching the mortuary express straight to heaven.

The fact was, their broken hearts would never mend. A hollow spot would have remained inside. They would have thought of me with confused mixtures of love and hate. Instead of leaving a tranquil sea of peace and joy, I would have left pain and sorrow for others to clean up and deal with.

For years I had trouble sorting out truth and fiction, reality and fantasy. Thank God the lies never won out.

I long for your salvation, O Lord,
and your law is my delight.
Let me live that I may praise you,
and may your laws sustain me.

PSALM 119:174-75

44

What Depression Taught Me

Depression is not a kindly professor who patiently teaches with the pupil's best interests at stake. It is a harsh, mean taskmaster, wearing the mask of a friend. The fact that depression sometimes benefits us is purely by accident, by our determination, and by the grace of God.

Beating yourself in the hand with a hammer has a certain amount of instructional value, but hardly enough to warrant the exercise.

As with most agonizing circumstances, wise is the person who learns from experience. The following are a few of the lessons I believe depression has inadvertently taught me.

1. I'm tougher than I thought. Usually we think that depression preys on the weak of mind or constitution. I did not begin to grow until I realized how strong one must be to survive the ravages of despair.

How does one weather the constant storms? The waves beating against the rocks? The seasick-like nausea? The uncertainty and darkness?

Anyone who has persevered through hurricane after hurricane has more experience and skills because of those experiences. Otherwise he wasn't paying attention.

2. I realize that even despair has its limits. Depression can all but destroy, but there is something inside that lives on. My soul or spirit continues, even if I fear it will not.

When the ashes in my fireplace look dark and still, there is often a surprise waiting beneath. Hot embers live on long after I have thought the fire was dead.

After the depression clears, a core inside me is found which still carries heat and light, enough for both this life and the next.

God made me that way and I have known it to be true.

3. Depression is sometimes a noisy bully. An old axiom served us as children: "If you fight a bully he is far less likely to battle you next time." Fighting a bully is hard. He is large, mean, and without conscience. But a bully doesn't really want to fight. If you smack him back a couple of times, he will go ahead and hurt you, but he won't be so quick to start a fight the next time.

Each time we fight depression, the depression becomes a bit weaker and a tad shyer.

When I see depression coming, and I frequently do, I have to decide to fight it off. And each time I fight it off, it has a little less power over me.

PART TWO

Why Shadows Grow So Long

A Wolf's Ghost

*Clinical depression is like a wolf's ghost that
sometimes returns to howl at my door.*
ELIZABETH BENKO

Many of us can relate to this woman's experience. Depression leaves its "scent." After a few visits, the old wolf's ghost has little trouble retracing its steps and finding our homes again.

Those who believe they have chased off the terrible monster only leave themselves wide open for its return. Mentally we build metal fences. We spray the path with fresh fragrances. We sound shots noisily into the air. But with all of that, we would be fools to think that the ghost could never again hide in the trees around our homes.

Whether that's good news or bad depends upon us. Hopefully the thought will lead us to respect the ghost. This will cause us to keep taking whatever precautions are necessary for our own protection and the protection of others.

*Meaning. Activity. Involvement. Creativity. Counseling.
Spirituality. Family. Friends. Medication.*

Those things that work to maintain mental health are the very things we must keep in good stead. Otherwise we will be tearing down our fences and inviting the elusive beast to howl again on our doorstep.

Caution is necessary for many of us. People with high blood pressure must show respect for their problem. Those who have had heatstroke need to keep an eye on the sun. Anyone with back problems must be careful when lifting. Sufferers of depression also must use caution.

Either we will hold the ghost of depression at bay or we will spend many nights lying awake, listening to it howl. Even if we are meticulously careful, the old wolf may steal more than its share of our joy.

Some feel like they have not only shot the wolf, but also successfully driven a stake through the ghost's heart. Surely a few have. They have earned our admiration. Unfortunately, most of us have not and never will. For us the call to careful vigilance must go on.

The price is well worth it. Those who have had months or even years without a visit from the beast know we have been smart to continue our watch. We do what it takes to keep our minds healthy and the ghost of depression at bay.

A Hole in My Head

Before I took better care of myself, I usually had one tooth or another that had a hole in it. Every so often a bit of sausage or piece of apple would find its way into this tiny cave and wedge itself tightly into position.

For hours I would suck at the intruder and try to vacuum out the morsel. Next, using my tongue as a prod, twisting it into various shapes and contortions, I would try to outsmart my unwelcome squatter.

Normally, after hours of struggle, I would win. An errant piece of food was sent hurtling to its destiny.

Unfortunately, the hole in my tooth never stayed vacant for long. At the next meal or the ever-present snack, a shard of pop-corn or peanut would wrest itself into the gap. I would start again.

Often I have wondered if a similar hole does not exist some-where in my head, my heart, or my psyche. If I am not careful, a dread darkness tries to take up residence inside me, as, for example, when a terrible thing that someone has said to me keeps repeating itself over and over. When I finally chase the need for approval away, almost immediately another bad thought takes its place.

My sense of inadequacy comes rushing in the minute the other culprit leaves. A day or two are spent wrestling with how poorly I measure up.

The hole in my tooth and the hole in my head each abhor a

vacuum. Neither remains empty for long. I don't know if this is a law of physics or a law of personality, but for me it's a fact of life.

Whatever the principle, one truth seems evident, in my experience. If I fill the hole (vacuum) with goodness, purpose, or meaning, there is no room for a dreadful visitor to take up residence.

If the hole must be filled, I (the owner) get first option at how to fill it. Supplying it with hope, happiness, or helping others is my best chance of keeping the varmints out. Most of us know it is easier to keep mental rodents away than it is to extricate them later.

Whether we are discussing teeth, heads, hearts, or souls, the analogy seems the same. When we fill them with timely, proper, and purposeful materials, they are less likely to become occupied with harmful substances.

Discouragement and despair are unwelcome in an occupied room.

> *You prepare a table before me*
> *in the presence of my enemies.*
> *You anoint my head with oil;*
> *my cup overflows.*

PSALM 23:5

Troubles Come Naturally

I can't understand it," a man in his thirties said. "I try to do everything right. I take classes. I give money away. I take care of my mother. But still things keep going wrong. You'd think things would go better."

Clearly he had come to believe that if he took care of "things," good fortune would follow him around and bad events would be kept away. He had read that, he had heard that, or he had been taught that somewhere.

What someone had failed to tell him was that trouble comes naturally. Pain, grief, loss, and despair are part of the human condition. Good people suffer. Bad people suffer. The book of Job teaches us, "Man born of woman is of few days and full of trouble" (Job 14:1).

Troubles are not reserved for the mean and evil. Neither is trouble kept from the righteous. Heartaches fall indiscriminately, on all kinds of people.

Many of us become discouraged because we don't expect bad to happen to us. Those who handle the agonies of life well seem to be those who accept disappointment as part of the journey.

Two types take life to extremes: (1) Those who expect life to be mostly fun, and (2) Those who expect life to be mostly pain. Generally our lives truck along somewhere in the middle.

Problem solving is a vital part of the human experience. We cannot afford to be angry at life simply because it presents obstacles. The person who feels fulfilled is the one who rises up and works through each situation.

"Why has turmoil fallen on me?" is the wrong question. Turmoil falls on all of us. The real question should be, "What can I do about the problem now?" The first question leads to self-pity and sadness. The second gives us hope to rise up and meet the need.

Once in a while we find someone who has experienced all kinds of setbacks: poor health, little money, an extra relative to take care of, and even more. Yet he or she has a level, calm outlook on life. He or she expects life to bring trouble. Instead of resenting it, this person grabs life in a headlock and wrestles it to the ground.

I like the spunk of Louisa May Alcott, who said she was "resolved to take Fate by the throat and shake a living out of her."

The Battle Continues

Tony hadn't taken a drink of alcohol in a decade or more. "To tell you the truth, though," he said, "I believe I could pick up a drink today and go back to it in a minute. Despite all the damage drinking did to me, it still sounds pretty good."

For many people, that which hurts them most—whether an experience, a thing, or a relationship—continues to hold power over them long after it is recognized as harmful. Even though it has badgered us, pierced our hearts, and left us crying in the night, it still holds a strong attraction, and keeps calling us back.

Tobacco can do it. Fast cars can do it. Gambling can do it. Sexual activity can do it. A need to control can do it. They may cost us our money, our health, our relationships, and our reputations, and yet these things still hold tremendous sway over our hearts and minds.

The same can be said of depression. Though depression may be ugly and nasty and destructive, it is still difficult to say goodbye to it forever. There may have been a time when we made uneasy peace with this beast. Still, if we found comfort in it, if we found safety, if we made deals with this devil, if we bargained with it, we might never totally free ourselves from its power.

Though there are long periods of tranquillity and even joy, temptation may return. If physical ailments or a family problem arises, if downsizing shrinks your income or your child gets into trouble, from the wings may come that haunting voice, calling you to come back. "Return to me," the tempter may whisper, "and find rest in me."

Why don't we simply tell it no? This is no simple matter. Depression, the Jezebel of feelings, has its own charms and attractions. It has a power that is hard to deny.

That's not to say that its power is irresistible. Fortunately, people overcome it everyday. But its power must be recognized and acknowledged. And when it returns, its victim must choose to fight it off yet another time.

Life is a battle. If we don't fight ants every year, they will take over the kitchen. If we don't take blood pressure pills, we are likely to have a stroke and be paralyzed. And if we do not pick up arms to resist depression from time to time, the monster may climb our walls again.

Those of us who have suffered dare not ignore its ongoing power.

When I said, "My foot is slipping,"
your love, O Lord, supported me.
When anxiety was great within me,
your consolation brought joy to my soul.

PSALM 94:18-19

55

Talking to My Adrenaline

After teaching a late-evening class, I was approached by one of the adult students, who told me how much she did *not* appreciate a point I had made in class. A small matter, I could barely remember saying it. And yet, when I arrived home, the lady's complaint still haunted me. I tossed, turned, and fumed all night.

The next day and night the remark continued to bother me. Another day. Another night. My condition didn't seem to improve.

Along the way I had one of those direct talks with myself. "Hey, this isn't worth it. I can't rest. I hate the woman." She had said nothing that warranted so much attention. I'm sure she had no idea how much her words had upset me. Why had the incident bothered me so much?

Eventually I figured it out. Since childhood I had lived on a bodily fluid called adrenaline, the old fight or flight chemical which our bodies naturally provide. Because most of my life had been spent in near panic, I needed this help to cope with my surroundings.

I had flunked tests repeatedly. I had seldom had decent clothes to wear. Bill collectors had come to our door. I had lied and deceived in order to exist. I had always felt out of place. Daily I had had to choose between fighting or fleeing.

My adrenaline had pumped so hard for so long that the supply line was now out of control. Any slight challenge caused my body to produce far more adrenaline than I needed at a given time.

When the lady in the class registered her objection, my adrenaline rushed in with its overload, and it stayed at that capacity for at least a week.

My mind knew the situation had ended, but my body couldn't catch on. To put it another way, my brain was apprehensive but my body remained in panic.

Once I came to the conclusion that my adrenaline was in flood stage, I began to take steps to keep it inside its banks. This is what I now do, with considerable success:

First, I talk to my adrenaline. "Slow down, old boy. This is a campfire, not a three-alarm." It needs to hear that.

Second, I de-reflect. De-reflection is a powerful force. Simply put, it means that I look for something else to do and think about. Go bowling. Read magazines. Take a hike.

Third, I try my best not to put two stressful encounters back to back. If routine stress can't be managed, maybe I should consider a major change, or perhaps even see a doctor.

The good news is, it is possible to do something about adrenaline flow. We can't control everything that happens to us in life, but we can manage our response to the things that bother us.

Not a Question of Character

As a child I wanted to be perfect. I knew I wasn't, but in my mind I assumed it was just a matter of time. Eventually I would be as fast, as goodlooking, and as smart as anyone. All I had to do was work harder, apply myself more, and focus more intently on my goals.

That's how I thought, but each passing year only proved how incorrect I was. Because I was never the fastest, never the brightest, reality began to settle in. The facts soon revealed a flawed person with considerable limitations.

Children can dream of boundless opportunities and imagine gifts they do not actually possess. As we grow older, we usually come to accept our natural abilities and limitations. That is, most adults recognize their strengths and weaknesses. Unfortunately, there are some who continue to hold on to childhood expectations.

Depression is a natural part of life. It can easily affect most of us, often without any fault of our own. Depression is not a reflection of our character. It's not that good guys are happy and bad guys get depressed.

Some of the finest people who have ever lived battled with serious bouts of depression.

Read that again.

We are now adults, and we are not perfect. That's the fact of the matter. Our sinuses sometimes drip, we are developing double chins, and we wear contacts. Those aren't character issues. Good guys get headaches. Bad guys get headaches.

We make the situation much harder to deal with if we believe depression is a question of character. This simply isn't true.

Once we say, "I am bad because I get depressed," the healing part becomes much more difficult. For many millions, depression is a condition that can be treated and usually improved. Depressed people have a problem, like an illness, and they need help.

Even good guys get depressed.

People and Dandelions

There are a great many dandelions in our neighborhood. A few lawns are totally green, while others, like mine, have enough golden flowers to cover a Rose Bowl Parade float. Some people get upset about dandelions. Some people don't.

Some homeowners are especially uptight over the problem. They apparently judge good people to be those who have nice lawns. The bad people are the ones who allow dandelions to dot the landscape.

People who worry about their neighbors' lawns are asking for trouble. They grind and burn inside because Neighbor X doesn't shape up. That kind of anger will eventually do damage.

Flowers or people? That shouldn't be a hard choice. What flower or weed should allow us to look down on people? When we start to dislike other people, it is easy to dislike ourselves as well.

Jonah had this problem. He didn't care about people, but he was very fond of a leafy plant that gave him shade. The Lord sent a worm to eat the stem of the plant, and the plant died.

Jonah was ticked. Was he angry about losing the plant? Very! That's when God gave him a lesson.

Jonah felt sorry for himself. The Lord said, "But there is a large city full of people who need help, and you don't care a whit about them." People or plants? Jonah was worried about the wrong thing.

Worry isn't what drives us bonkers. It is worry about the

wrong things. If worry causes us to do something helpful, then it serves a good purpose. But when worry is pointless, and when worry is destructive, all it really does is turn into harm.

There is good worry. If a bridge in the county looks weak, something should be done about it. Otherwise the school bus filled with children might crash into the creek.

But often we worry only about the weeds of life. Worrying about them leaves us tired and discouraged, and before long we become depressed, sweating the small stuff.

If we rise up, reach out to love, and accept people, we are far less likely to worry ourselves sick. We are foolish to worry about weeds.

How good and pleasant it is
when brothers live together in unity!

PSALM 133:1

Holidays Are Hard

Everyone is coming over for Thanksgiving. It's the all-American holiday. Relatives travel from afar, a spirit of festivity fills the air, and a good time will be had by all. What could be wrong with that? But the ideal picture is simply too threatening for some of us to handle.

Actually there isn't anything wrong with the traditional holidays. Getting rid of them would not make us feel better. The problem is that holidays tend to intensify everything. What is good in our lives seems to get better and what is wrong grows worse. Whether you like being with people or not, both are intensified.

Too often we think that the solution is to ignore holidays. That would be a pity. Instead, we need to look at ways to cope with the situation.

Get real! Forget the songs, movies, and paintings, where everything is perfect. Most families have a mixed bag during the holidays. Let the time be good and be happy with that.

Try to make others comfortable—within reason. Catering to everyone in order to make them think well of us will probably backfire. Be a thoughtful host or guest and then let it go. Relatives have responsibility for their own happiness.

Don't stay up late two nights in a row. It may be exhilarating to throw your system out of whack once, but twice is likely to affect the way you think. Energy, attitude, and chemistry are not to be toyed with for very long.

Pig out in moderation. This doesn't have to be contradictory. Enjoy the holiday feast. Don't feel guilty. But don't pig out for ten meals or three days. That might lead to digestive rebellion.

Take a walk. At our house you can watch them peel off, either alone or in groups of two or three, like giant seals looking for their own huge rocks. This people-in-your-face thing needs breathing room, no matter how large your house is.

Pitch in. Help set tables, do dishes, move chairs, anything that proves you aren't a total slug. The feeling that one's sole purpose over the next day or two is to scratch and belch will get most people down.

Don't try to resolve issues. If asked to lead in prayer, don't ask the Lord to make Uncle George return the money he borrowed three years ago. Settling scores gives holidays a bad name.

Be generous. Let others pick out television shows. Act like it doesn't matter who wins the touch football game.

Congratulate yourself for being a nice person and for reaching out to help others have a good time.

Flirting With Perfectionism

When it became apparent that Dan was not going to get an A in a class, he would drop it. After all, he reasoned, he was capable of all A's and would not compromise. In short order he was getting three A's, but he had dropped the other four classes. The ones he had dropped weren't up to his standard, so he had ditched them.

At this rate Dan was in a close race to see whether he would graduate or qualify for Social Security first.

In Dan's battle with depression he had decided that the only way to stay on top was to do everything perfectly. If everything he did was perfect, no one could criticize him and he could not criticize himself.

Some who suffer from depression seem to have "perfectionism" tattooed on their foreheads. Too many of us are depressed because we establish a standard of doing everything exactly right. We actually believe that the only ladder out of depression is to do everything perfectly.

Once we accept this value system, we are on a circular track leading to depression. The track looks like this:

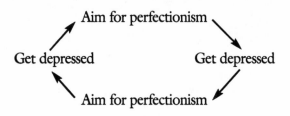

Like rats on a wheel, we run around and around but actually get nowhere. That's why we often feel run-down.

It's time to get off the track of perfectionism. In the middle of this futile race, simply stop running and walk off the field.

From now on I will aim for B's and C's. Then I'll take the rest of the day off, get a glass of iced tea, sit in the backyard, and read a book. Imperfection is good enough for me.

That doesn't mean I can't rise up to excellence. I can do an excellent job without being perfect. Perfectionism will never make me a complete person. Excellence is a valid goal. Perfectionism is a sickness.

Feeling Bad About Feeling Bad

What's the first thing you would you do if you fell out of a boat and into deep water, if you knew it would be some time before you would be rescued?

I'd take off my shoes. If I was wearing a sweater, I'd take that off, too. The added weight and bulk would make swimming or even dog-paddling difficult. In a life-threatening situation like that, I'd need all the energy I had, simply to stay afloat.

When we are depressed it's hard enough to keep our head above the water. Extra baggage pulls us under. Those of us who feel bad about feeling bad are wearing heavy shoes that drag us down.

The terrible propensity to feel down about being depressed seems particularly true of Christians. Somehow we have come to believe that we should be able to skip atop the waves of life. Testimonies tell us that. Books talk about victories. Radio shows tout the mountaintop experiences. We let ourselves believe that good people live free from anguish and disappointment. That's why we take setbacks so hard.

Loss, anxiety, stress, confusion, and depression are normal experiences. Why should any of us expect to escape the regular agonies of the average person? All of us suffer, though we may do so in different ways.

We dare not believe that God separates us and removes us from the human condition. We are not failures just because we have a number of very heavy burdens to carry.

Feeling bad about feeling bad has a great deal to do with feelings of guilt and shame. We somehow think pain should not come our way. Since it definitely does, we feel we must be doing something wrong to cause it. The truth is that pain will come our way no matter how hard we work to fend it off. Far better to concentrate on working through the trouble that has come than to spend our energy on feeling guilty.

Swimmers have a difficult time removing their shoes and shirts, once they have entered the water. Yet the odds of their survival are greatly increased once they have shed the extra, unnecessary burden. If we can likewise cast off our feelings of guilt, our odds of surviving—and ultimately conquering—depression are similarly increased.

He stilled the storm to a whisper;
the waves of the sea were hushed.
They were glad when it grew calm,
and he guided them to their desired haven.

PSALM 107:29-30

Dealing With Reality

A young man who lived on one side of town was deeply in love with a young lady on the other side of town. Unfortunately, the painful truth was that the young lady did not care for him.

The frustrated young man had a clear choice. He either had to change her mind or else change his own. If he refused to do either, he was doomed to disappointment.

Often we become angry because we don't accept reality. We want something to happen (we have an expectation); when it doesn't happen (reality), we get bent out of shape.

"Larry never calls."

"I didn't get a raise."

"My neighbor never apologized for the mess his dog made."

"I can't read fast enough."

"She won't go out with me."

"I am overweight."

"I can't fix the oven."

If we try to make something happen and it doesn't, what are our choices? If we can't change the situation, we must change ourselves. It's that simple. Those are the only two things that can change.

If Larry won't call, we need to be content without Larry. If the neighbor won't apologize, then we must change so that we don't need an apology. We eliminate frustration by changing our expectations. That's accepting reality.

A mother says she cannot be happy unless her son phones her regularly. Her son never does. She can become angry at her son and angry at life if she chooses. But why not accept reality and find other things to occupy her mind? That way she can cut back on her anger and emerge a happier and wiser lady.

"But," the mother objects, "I don't want to accept the fact that my son doesn't call." She denies reality. She will very likely become a bitter woman.

Make adjustments. Line up expectations with reality.

The ex-spouse is not coming back.

You will never be president of the company.

Your son will never play in the NBA.

A good definition of mental health is an acceptance of life as it really is. Anything else is too frustrating.

Surely you desire truth in the inner parts;
you teach me wisdom in the inmost place.

PSALM 51:6

Mental Traps

It starts off innocently enough. My wife asks me to go somewhere. It could be a picnic or a shopping trip. She certainly doesn't mean to set a trap, but in my mind it becomes one. No matter whether I decide to go or to stay, either will be a downer for me.

There is some strong reason why I don't want to go, and I feel badly that I "can't" go. At the same time, I feel terrible because I am going to stay home. Either way, I get down on myself.

I'm trapped. I'm no good if I go. I'm no good if I don't go. There is no clear way for me to get through this without feeling like crud.

This doesn't happen often, but when it does I go straight into the dumper. If you know me, you can see it in my face. Most of what you see is in my eyes, but there is also a gravity in my face and a slight change in my color. I've had several people mention the shift in my appearance.

I think of it as a trap because I believe I have no acceptable option. Whatever I choose will immediately result in my feeling miserable about myself and my self-worth.

Life can be whispering along very well when a choice like this comes out of the blue. I suspect that this mental trap is not peculiar to me. Most of us probably face unpleasant choices that leave us no attractive option.

It also seems obvious to me that my life will never be entirely trap-free. For those of us who suffer from depression, a few dangerous crevices will always be waiting, in which to fall and twist our psychological ankles.

There are definitely some situations we should avoid. Some people should not have caffeine. Still others have no business staying up late two nights in a row.

What shame is there in admitting that we do not handle some things well? Once in a while a situation will arise, no matter which way we turn. In that case we may have to take the damage, shake it off, and move on.

There is no safe place where nothing can get us. We should aim for relative safety, but that's the best we can do. The traps will come. We must explain our choice the best we can, rattle around, and keep on trucking.

Guilty of Being Me

Not long ago, at a gathering of friends, I said something really dumb. It was crass; it was rude; it was goofy. The minute the words came tumbling out, I wanted to suck them back in, chew them up, and swallow them.

All of us have done something like that. It's natural and normal. Kind of like spilling food.

However, not everybody takes it to the next step. This is the one that gets me into trouble. Instead of getting down on what I have said, I get down on who I am. In a nanosecond I decide I am stupid, useless, and despicable. No one wants to be around me; no one has any use for me. I continue to spiral downward. By midnight I am wondering why I don't find a train to jump in front of.

Many people don't go to this extreme, and certainly not this quickly. But some of us do. Like fine clothing, we feel any mark on it renders it useless, and impulsively we want to throw it away. The only problem is, we are talking about people and not fabric. Specifically, I am talking about me.

Over the years I allowed the distance between a dumb action and my total self-rejection to become as short as a millimeter. I'd say something unkind and go straight to rejection. Sort of, "I did bad equals I am bad," and just about that swiftly.

Once we get into a rejection cycle, the loop gets smaller and smaller. Soon we have no tolerance for any of our mistakes or misdeeds. No longer can we tolerate any hint of imperfection in ourselves.

In my case, it was as if I could accept my own imperfection as long as it was not specific. The minute I or anyone else pointed out exactly where I fell short, I plummeted directly into self-rejection. Walking on so thin a ledge was a precarious existence indeed.

My yo-yo string was too short. The string was tangled and the yo-yo could not go about its normal routine. Life on a short string was tough.

Consciously and deliberately I needed to unravel the twisted mess that inhibited me. I needed more string.

Slowly I learned to give myself more tolerance in allowing for my own mistakes. I learned that if I kept the string too short, life moved in jerks and jolts rather than singing along.

Tolerance is the key. I have the right to do dumb things. And when I do them I must forgive myself, accept myself, and continue singing along.

The Seven O'Clock Wall

A number of people I have known, including myself, have experienced the seven o'clock wall. It doesn't happen every evening, but the pattern is worth noting.

When the clock lights up at seven, a crisis of undetermined proportions begins. What will I do for the evening? The decision is even more intense on Friday or Saturday nights.

Many people have trouble choosing what to do in the evenings, but in a person experiencing this problem, the very choice is critical. Not having anything scheduled and not being able to pick an activity sends some of us into a panic.

The problem is twofold. First, we believe that there are plenty of interesting places to go and things to do. Second, we believe that we cannot make a good decision or create a worthwhile evening.

Frozen, we feel unable to call a friend, work on our hobby, or go out the door. People who are frozen cannot punch out a phone number.

For one hour, from 7:00-8:00 P.M., true turmoil rages through our minds and bodies. We fight depression, grow bold, shift back to fear, and experience true trauma. Yet when the clock turns to 8:00 our bodies calm down and our fears are allayed, like a balloon stretched almost to the point of bursting and then deflating to a reasonable size.

The reason the crisis subsides at eight o'clock is because by that time we believe most choices have now passed. It's too late to start a project, too late to call anyone. Since our decisions have been narrowed, we can adjust to a safe evening. And we are relieved.

This is not normal decision making. This is genuine crisis. We hit the seven o'clock wall and go into a quiet panic.

Having broken the barrier at 8:00 P.M., we sit down with a book, watch TV, or turn on our computer. The terribly wide variety of possibilities from which to choose has shrunk to a manageable few.

While that one hour of true tension passes, we are tortured by the process. Some of us go through this regularly. I suspect that many do.

It helps to know what is going on. We know it will pass. If we make plans early in the day, we often can avoid the crisis altogether.

Where the Internet Can Lead

How could the internet affect mental health and social well-being? There are studies that suggest people like us could stumble into the darkness if we use the internet too often. And people like us tend to use it too often.

My love for trivia began in a similar way. As a child I withdrew socially and made friends with an old encyclopedia. While I was flunking school, at home I was reading about vice presidents, European wars, and the history of coal mining. My version of home-schooling regularly ran late into the night and spilled over into the morning.

Today the internet could probably serve the same purpose. I could spend long evenings avoiding people and researching the migratory habits of the Monarch butterfly. Frankly, I would love it.

The problem is that evidently among those who soak up endless facts (or factoids) there is a high rate of depression. That evidence shouldn't shock us. All the ingredients seem in place: isolation, loss of contact, lack of give-and-take, disconnection with reality.

When a group of internet users were tested over a period of time, increased use and increased depression were in direct proportion. Likewise, these people showed an increase in loneliness and a decrease in social contacts as their level of internet usage increased.

Which comes first: depression or increased internet usage?

The most important fact is that they may be traveling hand in hand. If one's best friend is a machine, maybe one should be concerned.

The computer is not the enemy. An electronic box is not the cause of my troubles. It cannot have power over me or cast a hex on my life. A machine has only the powers I assign it.

Millions are able to control their use of the internet and set proper limits. Yet some of us do a poor job of establishing boundaries. If that happens, the system can be allowed to hurt our marriages, relationships with our children, or contacts with others.

If we feel like people really don't like us, if we would rather interact with a computer most of the time, if we feel down and drained after extended use, if the people we love are complaining about the competition, these may be flashing danger lights which we can't afford to ignore.

More and more people are seeking counseling because of "computer problems." When the people and computers clash, it's better if people win.

The Fear of Thankfulness

Whenever I feel like a big, first-class, all-time loser, it seems like someone will say, "Remember, you have a lot to be thankful for."

I hate that. People have some gall telling me I should be grateful. Don't they realize how dreadful my situation has become?

At times like that, I don't want to be thankful. This is because I know the truth. Being thankful is a life preserver. If someone tosses it to me and I grab it, I will be rescued from depression. I sense that. That is why I choose to swim away from gratitude.

Depression and thankfulness are incompatible. It's hard to think of anyone who has shown signs of both at the same time. Gratitude means we are up. Depression means we are down. How many of us can travel both directions at once?

Consciously, overtly, I can see the medicine bottle sitting in front of me, and I refuse to take it. This is partly because I know it will work, and I don't want it to. In this case the "medicine" is recognizing and emphasizing how many things I can be grateful for.

Often, depression, like suicide, is the great deceiver. It convinces me to do the exact opposite of what I know will work for me. I know that thankfulness can cause me to smile, to care, and to hope, and I do not want to do any of those things. So I tell myself it won't work, and I run away.

I cried for a life preserver. And when one was thrown my way, I swam away from it.

Even if we don't want to hear it, we know that thankfulness is a potent antidote. When we are grateful for health, children, hobbies, faith, work, friends, or whatever, depression becomes all but paralyzed.

In order to feel better we must be willing to do better. If we are thankful, we will then feel better. Don't wait to feel thankful.

One good way is to draw a double circle in the shape of a life preserver. Then write down two or three things for which you are grateful. That's a beginning. It's a first step in admitting the fact that some things are better in life than you want to admit.

Sacrifice thank offerings to God,
fulfill your vows to the Most High,
and call upon me in the day of trouble;
I will deliver you, and you will honor me.

PSALM 50:14-15

Where's the Loss?

Betty felt depressed because she had lost the innocence of her childhood. Sexually abused at eight years of age by a man who lived next door, she always knew there was something lost from her life. She had not misplaced her innocence; the neighbor had stolen it away. After the initial theft, he came back again and again, proving he owned the keys to the door.

Betty's depression was an attempt to deal with loss. Love and her sense of security had been taken from her early in life.

Some people have lost a person or relationship, others have lost an opportunity or a dream. Occasionally what they lost was something that was not guarded carefully enough: a scholarship, a romance, or the near-perfect job.

With me it was the loss of my childhood. I felt cheated out of joy, acceptance, safety, and even creativity. There was no island where I was free to test and see who I really was. Threats entered my home and lived in its rooms. My bedroom was not private. The living room was volatile and ready to explode at any moment. The kitchen and dining room had a stranger in residence. The back room was the place where my father hid and slept. Nowhere was I wanted. Nowhere could I develop. Nowhere did I learn the normal give-and-take of life.

This was genuine, deep loss, not superficial deprivation. In no sense did I feel that at any given moment I was a complete person.

Later in life I needed to learn to deal with my loss. I needed to parent the child who never was. Consciously I looked for places to belong. Purposefully I tried to connect to the people I valued. Objectively I searched for avenues where I felt capable and confident. If my parents could not or would not give security to me, I had to supply it for myself.

There had to be a way to address the loss. Was I to compensate for it? Was I to accept the loss as irretrievable? Was I to move on and help heal the loss in others? All of these were possible to some extent. And all helped me to minimize the effects of that loss in my life, so that I would not be so susceptible to anger and depression.

Gratefully, I began to give myself credit for who I was and what I could do. I started to appreciate how valuable I was in God's collection of people. By God's grace I was worthwhile, and now I simply needed to accept it.

> *I waited patiently for the Lord;*
> *he turned to me and heard my cry.*
> *He lifted me out of the slimy pit,*
> *out of the mud and mire;*
> *he set my feet on a rock*
> *and gave me a firm place to stand.*

PSALM 40:1-2

Shutting Down

In the movies, when a submarine is damaged during battle, it drops down below the action and waits until the enemy goes away. With depth charges blowing up around it, airplanes dropping bombs, and huge guns blasting, the submarine crew knows it can't cope under such overwhelming circumstances. Consequently, the submarine shuts down, and quietly sinks away.

Though I no longer have the dark periods of depression I used to have, I still occasionally have "submarine" depression. Unable or unwilling to deal with today's difficulties, I drop down, or depress myself, for a while, until the things that are troubling me go away.

This is voluntary, conscious depression. I choose this because it seems safe. If I go someplace and sulk, if I don't talk to anyone and I refuse to be cheerful, I can escape for an hour or two.

I will eventually come out of my dark mood, and I am aware of that when I go into my dive. But at that moment I believe survival is too painful, possibly even too risky, if I stay on the surface.

Controlled depression is a learned pattern of behavior. No one taught it to me. I experimented with the device as a young child. As sad and dismal as it is, it seemed like a better alternative than facing hard and sometimes cruel reality.

The good news is that when I recognized these particular bouts of depression as voluntary, I also realized that coming out of them was just as easily managed. Unless, of course, I dove too deeply. Then I was in danger of losing control over my ability to revive myself.

Depression is always a dangerous place to visit. Visitors run the risk of losing their way and not being able to return when they like.

Early in the "voluntary" process, depressing may work for us. If we stay too long, however, we may lose our way and become a slave to the depression.

Addicted to Self-Help

When you first taste a cough lozenge, you enjoy the candy flavor. The coughing seems to subside, and soon you take another. Why not take a lot if such painless medicine accomplishes so much? Numbers four, five, and six are soon consumed and your nasal passages are as dry as a wicker basket.

Then, and only then, do you accidently read the warning label. "Too many might cause constipation." That little fact comes as a surprise, but by now those drops have a hypnotic draw. What's a little constipation, you figure, when the flavor is so tantalizing?

Self-help books and tapes are a direct analogy. The first one you pick up is packed with practical advice and clever information. The knowledge proves very helpful. You praise the material.

However, since the self-help book was beneficial but did not cure all of your difficulties, the next step seems obvious enough. Read a second book. Read a third one. And then read an exhausting fourth volume.

As with the cough drops, side effects begin to set in. Something akin to constipation. Advice, advice, advice. Steps, formulas, phrases, and key words begin to pile up. Soon it is time to get a fifth book to help sort all of this out.

Before long you no longer trust your common sense. You no longer know how to think without a fix from another book. You have developed a dependency on self-help books. You become aware that you are "mentally constipated."

How many people go to a counselor, worn out from reading about their purported mental illness or relational problems? For all the good in self-help books, there is a place at which guidelines begin to back up on us.

Read one good self-help book. If necessary, try a second. But if the problem persists, don't read a third. Go to the phone and seek help from a good counselor.

Change the Pattern

Suppose a gentleman eats breakfast at a certain restaurant every day. Every morning he enters the diner, paper in hand, and sits at the same place at the same table in the corner of the room. Same order, every time: two eggs over easy. Toast. Tomato juice. He eats his breakfast as he reads the paper. Every day for ten years it's the same thing.

Now, imagine one day he comes in and sits in his normal place. Reads the paper, eats his eggs ... and when he stands to leave, he hits his head on a recently installed overhead cabinet. For a second the gentleman recoils with pain, then he leaves with a stinging headache.

Naturally, it hurt the gentleman when he rapped his skull on wood. However, the next morning he returns to the same table and when he rises to leave he hits his head again. How many times would he have to hit his head on the cabinet before he adjusted his regular routine? It wouldn't take much to change the pattern. He wouldn't have to give up his favorite diner, or even change his order to pancakes. All he really would have to do is switch to another table. But since he has occupied that same corner for ten years, this solution doesn't occur to him. Instead, he continues to hit his head every morning.

Millions of us are caught in unhealthy patterns. We've been doing the same thing for years and are unwilling to make a change. Instead, we keep taking the lumps on our psychological craniums.

A man I know goes bowling once a week with a friend. That friend is highly critical. He tells the man he has the wrong ball; that he stands too far to the left of center; and that he shouldn't bend over so far.

Every week this man goes home feeling defeated and depressed. Yet, the next Tuesday, there he is, at 7:30 P.M. sharp, ready to take another mental whipping from his friend.

Why doesn't he change the pattern? He could tell the man to stop criticizing him. If that didn't work, he could stop bowling with the guy and take up pigeon raising. He could even choose to sever the relationship.

Yet, almost mesmerized, like the proverbial moth, this man is drawn to the flame. He cannot wake himself up and say, "Hey, I don't like what's happening to me."

Does a television show get you down? Is eating breakfast alone turning into a bummer for you? Is your mother-in-law driving you bonkers? Can you identify an unhealthy pattern in your life? Do what it takes to change the pattern and to walk in the sunshine again.

Never Owned a Gun

Every now and then hunting sounds good to me. Walking in the woods with a bunch of guys, sitting by a fire telling jokes—all of that camaraderie stuff is something I'd like to try. But the idea of owning a gun is a bit more than I can undertake.

I've spent some time shooting and I like it. I enjoy setting up a few cans and passing an afternoon blowing up clay pigeons. It's fun.

Most of the time a rifle or pistol would be perfectly safe in my house. Yet something in the back of my mind says, "Don't mess with anything that might be too handy in a sudden impulse." Why should I have something around that I am not sure I could always handle?

To some extent, the fear of owning a gun reminds me that I am not totally well. So be it. I seldom feel completely healed. Depression is like an old habit that could return when I least expect it. I have developed a healthy respect for it, and I don't care to raise the stakes too high.

There is no way to make my house or my car absolutely safe. In fact, a gun is quite possibly only a symbol. Still, it is a powerful symbol. In one stupid moment I could do something that would wreck a lot of people's lives. Not to have a gun seems like the best route.

Has depression robbed me of many happy hours in the field, stomping around with a good old buddy? It's a small price to pay. If I can't handle gambling, I ought to leave it alone. If alcohol is a threat, I should walk a wide swath around it. That's solid sense. The sacrifice of a weapon is no sacrifice at all.

Whenever I read a newspaper article about someone who has killed himself with a gun, I pause for just a few seconds. I think, "If he had gotten rid of the gun, he might still be here today." If at that sad impulsive moment there had been no rifle in the house, he might be working on issues in a counselor's office today. Instead, his family is grieving in a funeral home.

Those of you who ride the jerky tracks of depression might do well to get rid of your weapons. You won't be able to shoot doves this season or line up cans on the back fence. But you might be around a few more seasons to watch your children grow up.

It's a small price to pay.

PART THREE

Heading for the Sunshine

Hear my cry, O God;
listen to my prayer.

From the ends of the earth I call to you,
I call as my heart grows faint;
lead me to the rock that is higher than I.

For you have been my refuge,
a strong tower against the foe.

I long to dwell in your tent forever
and take refuge in the shelter of your wings.

Selah.

PSALM 61:1-4

Seasons of Depression

For most of us, February is dark, dull, and cold. Getting out takes extra effort and added clothing. The darkness seems to mess with our minds, and spring seems far away. Sports fans see it as the sports doldrums. Football is officially over and baseball camp won't get into swing until March.

Millions of us are engulfed by depression during certain seasons. Holidays send some of us into a sad funk. Birthdays put the whammy on quite a few. Even tax season leaves many of us without the will to fight. There are different mixes for different folks.

Don't be surprised if April or May throws you into the dumper. Some people survive the dark months of winter by telling themselves that everything will get better when the weather improves. Then they will go swimming, boating, and barbecuing, and play beach volleyball. All of that sounds terrific.

Depression sets in when spring begins to open the tulips, and those people fail to find new life. The seasons change and they are still lonely, sad, and despondent. Then they must admit that the weather change did not do the trick. These people must find another way to raise their spirits.

For others, summer is a tough time. Lovely weather turns into oppressive heat, and we retreat to our basements in search of cooler air and go outside as seldom as possible.

One person's up time is another's down time. We have different personalities; different chemistry. Who can be sure what all the contributing factors might be?

One way to combat seasonal depression is to map out the year. It might be helpful to do this with a friend, spouse, or counselor. What months seem to bring the most sadness into your life? Can you discover a pattern? When you do this, ask yourself what you might do to change your setting or your situation during that time.

Now you are being proactive. You're taking charge and doing something about your problem.

During your "bad season," take a trip. Join a team. Call a friend more frequently. Take a painting class. Leave more lights on in your house. Play cheerful music.

Don't settle for being a victim of the calendar. Things do not need to be as they have always been. Determine to break the old mold.

Mountains and Valleys

None of us are able to skip along the mountaintops of life. That's what I wanted to do, and I was terribly disappointed when I found I couldn't. The sad fact is that valleys separate the mountains, and we all come down from time to time. That's normal.

No one illustrates the point better than an ancient prophet named Elijah. His story helps a great deal—you can read it for yourself in 1 Kings 18–19. Here we find that Elijah had challenged the prophets of Jezebel to a showdown. The 450 prophets of Baal and the 400 prophets of Asherah made a sacrifice of dead bulls, while Elijah also made a sacrifice. Then each of them prayed, asking their deity to consume the sacrifice with fire.

Elijah's God came through.

Elijah was delighted at the decisive victory until Queen Jezebel and King Ahab sent troops to find and kill him. Scared spitless, Elijah ran off to the desert near Beersheba to hide.

Tired, disappointed, and hungry, he sat down and prayed that God would let him die. (This sounds like depression to me.) Though Elijah had recently been on a mountain peak, he found that he couldn't stay there.

Nestled under a tree, the prophet soon fell asleep. We don't know how long he slumbered, but an angel touched him, "all at once."

"Get up and eat," an angelic messenger told him. A cake of

baked bread and a jar of water lay by his head. (I've always imagined it was really a huge cinnamon roll with double icing and a glass of cold lemonade.)

Elijah ate the food, reached for the snooze button, and went back to sleep. The angel nudged him again, and he woke to eat once more. (I imagine this time he ate a chocolate eclair and drank a glass of milk.) From this nourishment Elijah was able to travel forty days and forty nights.

This story is a great example of God's faithfulness, but it also has some important lessons for us on how to cope with depression. Every once in a while I hit a great mountaintop. Things go extra well and I surf along the peak. Then suddenly I dip drastically down into the valley. It's then that I wonder how goofy I must be.

The truth is that without valleys there are no mountains. Life is not an endless plain with no ups or downs. There is joy and there is pain.

Heroes like Elijah make a difference. He had many dimensions and colorful sides. His life says volumes about the roller coasters we ride along the way.

Our Parents Did It

Depression is not like male pattern baldness. We don't get angry because grandfather did. Each of us makes decisions about what our mood will be and how we might control it. As someone said, "If we get sick and tired of being sick and tired, we will look for a way to do something about it."

If a parent suffered from depression, we may have a propensity to depress, but seldom is it inevitable. Granted, the twig may be bent in a certain direction, but human twigs are rerouted all the time.

Moody parents frequently have cheerful children. Cheerful parents may well have a pouty, unpleasant two-year-old. We all make choices that rise above our parental environment. Hang in there and deal thoroughly with your faults.

The children of soldiers can become poets. Pastors' sons can race automobiles. Postal workers can give birth to biologists. We are not bound to imitate Mom or Dad.

The problem of depression is mine. I claim it as my own. To understand my mother's depression or my grandfather's depression is only a little help. There are other, equally important, aspects of my own behavior that I must understand, and questions that I must ask.

Do I presently have a mood problem?

Do I have a chemical imbalance?

How can I adjust my attitude?

Why do I get angry?

How can I add genuine meaning and purpose to my daily existence?

There are far more significant issues than trying to allocate blame.

Our health will improve as we take responsibility for our own development. There may be important issues we want to discuss with our parents, but finding help is *our* job. Healthy people do something about their own depression.

Jesus Worked It Out

The Bible says Jesus Christ was "troubled." There is no suggestion that he was clinically depressed, but it's evident that some things got him down. Why wouldn't they? He was in the heat of the battle against evil. Sometimes it must have seemed like a terrible struggle.

In some sense, he is like me and I am like him.

Jesus described himself as "overwhelmed with sorrow to the point of death" (Mt 26:38). Why didn't he simply grin and bear his problems? Because some problems are tremendously difficult to handle, and Christ was dealing with the most difficult.

Understandably, Jesus asked for some relief under the enormous pressure. He asked the heavenly Father to cancel this trip. If possible, he wanted out.

Not all of his problems were centered on death, sacrifice, and God's will. Some were people problems and the failures of others. He asked the disciples, "Could you men not keep watch with me for one hour?" (Mt 26:40).

People and their fickleness got to him. It bothered him that even those who were supposed to be most committed to the cause—his disciples—could not be counted upon. After finding them asleep, Jesus went aside and again asked the Person in charge to scrap the project. Then he came back to find the disciples deeply committed to a long nap.

Jesus was getting down, and it showed. He was sorrowful,

troubled, vacillating, irritable, perplexed, and impatient. And he was the Son of God.

Thanks, Jesus. I needed that. Even though our trials are a million miles apart, they are also very similar. It's good to know that sometimes people and problems got to you. On a smaller level, they get to me, too.

Obviously you worked it out. You hashed over the obstacles, expressed yourself, and then decided to complete the sacrifice. I am grateful that you faced the problem head-on and paid the price in full for me.

You showed me that even the strong have difficulties, and even the best people must sometimes suffer. Sometimes my difficulties seem like too much to handle. It helps to know that you, too, had very tough days and yet you worked through them.

Some days that's precisely the reminder I need.

Help Will Work

One of the hardest obstacles for me to get over was believing that help was possible. I thought that anyone in my condition and circumstances would have to suffer forever. I was a million miles from truth.

Two facts seem inescapable. First, most people who seek help from a professional see their condition improve. Depression is highly treatable. A counselor can help find the cause or causes of depression. Most people who receive counseling find relief and experience greater satisfaction in life.

The second fact is that even with the improvement, the majority of us will need to keep a careful eye on depression for the rest of our lives. Yet watching out for it is a far better alternative than being overwhelmed by the intruder.

It is hard to give in and see a counselor. It's like saying, "I am starving and there is food on the other side of the creek. But if I walk through the creek my feet will get wet, I will chill, I might slip on a rock, a fish might nibble my toe, a storm could come up, and lightning is likely to strike me if I am standing in the water. Besides, someone might bring the food to me here."

The thought of going for help is similar. If I go to a counselor it will cost me money, take time from work, and hurt my pride. The counselor will soon find out how weak I am, that I have dirty thoughts, that I can't spell, and that I hate my Aunt Audrey. In short order he or she will know that I am as useless as I think I am. He or she will describe my character flaws and insist that I do something that I am scared to death to do.

There's something else to consider, too. It's one thing to let a stranger in on the secret. But what if my family and coworkers find out that I am in counseling? Then they, too, will know I am weird.

All these realities make people hesitant to make that first call. But it's important to weigh all of those excuses against fact number one: Most people who seek a counselor for help with depression find it.

Still, we don't go. It's regrettable. It's painful. It's a sad waste. It's understandable. Yet, no pain, no gain.

You have to admire the many people who take that risk, rise above their fears, and reach out for help. In the end, everyone has a different reason for doing it. Some do it for themselves, for their families, or for their spouses. Whatever the reason, they find the courage to look for a little peace of mind.

Time Zone

Often it's the little, unexpected things that bring healing and health to our lives: a throwaway sentence here, an off-the-cuff statement there. Like wonders in the forest, we come upon them unexpectedly.

During a conversation with a friend this tiny gem was tossed out. "Bill," he said, "you keep getting out of your time zone."

That simple, direct comment has had a profound effect on my mental health of the past decade. Before that I had tremendous trouble living in the "now." My mind was constantly spread into next month. And when it wasn't trying to deal with tomorrow, my attention was called back by the haunting voices of the past.

No wonder I had no energy for today. How could I possibly concentrate on this afternoon when I had not yet figured out what I was going to do next Christmas or why last Christmas was such a bore?

My friend didn't tell me what to do. Rather, he challenged me to rethink an ugly habit. That habit had stampeded my mind in all directions and had prevented me from drinking in the moment.

Previously I would crash and be despondent all weekend, worrying about Monday. Today I am more likely to have a bit of a chat with myself. "Hey, Coleman," I will say, "look what you're doing. You are ruining today—this moment—by trying to live in tomorrow. Get back into your time zone. You can deal with Monday on Monday."

Most of the time it works. Seldom do I become paralyzed trying to unravel the fears of next February.

In the Sermon on the Mount Jesus Christ put it simply.

Therefore do not worry about tomorrow,
for tomorrow will worry about itself.
Each day has enough trouble of its own.

MATTHEW 6:34

Next fall I am scheduled to speak at a conference. But, hey, that's next fall. It's time to pull in my worry antennae and go for a long afternoon drive with my life partner.

No Leapfrogging

It happens all the time. Someone has a problem, and instead of dealing with the specifics, the individual leapfrogs over it and moves on. Leapfrogging can be a good approach once in a while, but often it merely allows us to avoid dealing with the issues that need to be handled.

Leapfrogging is one of the difficulties with mood-changing medications. A godsend in some situations, in others medications help us escape the hurt, and we never make the changes that need to be made. The failure to work our way through our problems will probably create even greater trouble further down the line.

When a person grieves the loss of a loved one, heartache and agony can be excruciating. But how helpful is it to take medicine which might make one euphoric and prevent one from working it through?

This is almost to say that we should not grieve or suffer the pain of loss, but merely take medication and get beyond that feeling. Did your wife die? Go ahead and grieve. Ache. Spend some sleepless nights. Piddle with your meals for a while. It is normal to grieve a spouse. Only when the grieving process becomes too long or too twisted might you want to seek intrusive medication to help you leapfrog.

Medication has its place. I have recommended that some clients see their doctors about getting medicine. But more often there are issues to work through.

On the other side are those with clear signs of depression who ask for medication. When medicine makes them feel better, they are no longer interested in working on unresolved issues that may have caused the despair in the first place.

Look at this cycle. A woman is depressed and goes for counseling. The counselor sends her for medication. The medication helps her feel better, so she quits counseling. Eventually the medicine is too boring or too expensive, so she stops taking it. The following month she goes back to the counselor. What was the help in that?

Some depression is normal.

- your teenage daughter is pregnant
- your husband has left you for another woman
- the boss has threatened to fire you

Why shouldn't you be depressed?

There is a need for counseling for some. There is a need for medication for some. Either way, there is a need to work through problems instead of leapfrogging.

The Flickering Flame

Cindi had trouble with the flame of courage. She could turn on the gas and go after her dream at times, but she was highly susceptible to the winds of discouragement. If someone said her dream was a lousy idea, her flame began to flicker immediately. If a friend frowned or looked terribly concerned, Cindi's fire would soon go out.

Going back to school may have been exactly what she needed. Cindi collected the literature, saved money, and was preparing to quit her job and take the plunge. Then she talked to her sister. Her sister's brow wrinkled with worry. Her hands tightened into fists.

Before long, Cindi reevaluated her status. Within two weeks she gave up the idea and submerged herself in a humdrum job with no space to dream.

It wasn't that Cindi didn't have the fire. It wasn't that Cindi couldn't get started. The problem was, once she got a fire going, at the slightest sign of discouragement Cindi let the flame go out. She dumped a pail of water on her own fire.

Many of us are like this young lady. We lack the enthusiasm and the mental stamina to keep our plans alive. If someone opens the window, maybe only a crack, a breeze extinguishes our flame.

Our friends are not at fault. They may merely have asked questions or wondered out loud. That was enough to douse our dream.

Mental toughness is hard to maintain if depression is our companion. Seeing something clearly and then carrying it through are difficult if self-doubts and sadness walk beside us. Too often we take a detour.

The good news is that mental toughness, like physical toughness, grows by exercise. The more we hold on to our dreams, the easier it becomes to hold on the next time.

It might help to keep a record of how often we start a project and see it through, no matter what. Someone dumps cold water on us. All manner of skeptics come along and kick at our dream, hoping to knock it over.

The more often we see it through, the tougher our mind will become. We will not be easily discouraged if we take responsibility for making our own plans work.

Give It a Rest

One of the reasons I like movies so much is that they give me a chance to de-reflect. For two hours I get lost in sound, scene, and story. My problems don't go away, but for a time they no longer control my thoughts. If I couldn't de-reflect, I would concentrate too much on the challenge and dig a huge hole.

Sometimes I have thought that de-reflection is a bad thing. After all, I argue with myself, a guy ought to fight his battles through and stare them down. But staring at a problem too long causes it to grow larger and fill up the room.

When I drive east along the highway at daybreak, the sun hits my windshield and blinds me. If I choose, I can simply stare right back at it. But who will win this staring contest? The sun always does. However, if I use my visor to block the sun, if I look off to one side to avoid the direct light for a few miles, or if I use sunglasses, I can reduce the obstruction and still move forward.

This is a small price to pay to find relief for a time.

Unfortunately, millions use destructive ways to de-reflect. They use drugs, get drunk, take terrible chances. Often they make matters worse.

Unlike escapism, de-reflection makes this clear statement: My present difficulties are not my entire existence. They are part of me. They are not the total.

Movies aren't the only way to find help. Some people

immerse themselves in projects. It's also good to keep a "diversion book" around. This kind of book has to have the right balance for me. It must contain some new knowledge, yet not too much. It has to be highly readable, but not so light that I don't care what's going on. A "diversion book" is a fine tool to help clean out the brain for an hour or two. That bit of derailment is just enough to let me get back on track and continue my journey.

The person who distrusts de-reflection travels the journey the hard way. Everything is serious. Everything is head-on. Everything is direct. Every windshield takes the sun's full force.

Wholesome de-reflection is a present we give ourselves because we care enough to protect our mental health. Those who use it well are more likely to keep themselves together.

Counseling Takes Courage

Four times I found myself in a counselor's office seeking help for one thing or another, five times if you count premarriage counseling. Each and every time it took courage. More courage than I thought I could muster, but somehow it bubbled to the top.

Now it is obvious to me how brave a person has to be to lift the phone, punch out the numbers, and actually speak to whoever takes the call. Showing up at the office is equally difficult.

I always felt the counselor knew everything about me. He or she knew why I shook hands the way I did and why I combed my hair with a part. Somehow he or she could decipher my words and know the deep, dark reasons why I was talking quickly or slowly.

I thought the counselor knew that I was scared to death.

Coward is a useless word when it comes to counseling, so let's get rid of it. The title is dark and ugly and only confuses those who say or hear it.

This much I know. Most of us who show up in a counselor's office had to "gird up our loins," swallow our pride, and take a considerable risk. But millions of us are glad we took that precarious step forward.

Today counseling is popular, and even borders on the faddish for some. Because of this many have received help with depression, stress, marriage, child care, and a host of other problems.

It feels good to know that avenues are open to help when we know we need it.

Unfortunately, too often we wait until a catastrophe happens before we pick up the phone. Late is better than never, but sooner would have been best. If we know we have a problem and that problem seems to be getting worse, it is wise to take a bold step forward. We step out of the mud before we sink further.

Discussing the Loss

Gail didn't want to talk about her failing health. "That's the way life is," she insisted. "All of us lose our health and eventually we die. No one wants to listen to somebody whine about her problems."

There is nothing wrong with parts of what Gail had to say. But put together, her statements don't add up correctly. If we can't discuss our losses, we are very likely to repress them and go into some form of depression. Talking out our losses helps us recover from our grief.

Sadness often comes from some type of loss. We no longer have a companion or a comfortable financial outlook or the flexibility we've always enjoyed. Our lives feel diminished by these losses. We grieve over what is missing. We become angry, and when this lasts too long it degenerates into full-blown depression.

Healthy people "talk out" some of that loss. Otherwise they become focused on their hurt. Later they could become obsessed by it.

There are two separate questions: First, how can you get rid of the pain? Second, how can you go on with life if the pain won't go away? The first may not have a good answer. The second has several real possibilities.

What about whining? Whining means all I do is complain to everyone about my situation, and I do it at the drop of a hat. Whining is unattractive and boring. Sharing pain is different from whining. Sharing is done selectively. Meaningful discussion is limited by who we talk to and how often.

Good friends want to hear about our hurts. They are concerned, loving, and kind. Healthy people should be able to find one or two such friends and explain to them how they feel. By discussing loss with a good listener, we usually avoid the miserable trap we call depression.

Can Chocolate Heal?

The leader of the group asked its members to discuss what they do to help pull out of depression. After meeting in pods they reassembled, and the first person to volunteer information said succinctly:

"It's chocolate. No doubt about it. I bet every woman in this room would say the same thing."

That may be the best news we've received in years. Maybe decades. Chocolate could be a temporary cure for depression for millions of us.

Johns Hopkins University doesn't have to do years of research for me. There is plenty of evidence walking around on Main Street. Who really doubts that a quick candy bar, a handful of chocolate-coated peanuts, or a couple of chocolate-covered donuts will do the trick? The very thought of it gets your toes tapping and your cheeks grinning. Deny it if you can.

Who has not sat sulking and blue, wondering which way to turn, when his or her eyes locked onto a package of double chocolate candy cups? How often did that silly treat make you not only want to live again, but also grab the world by its polar caps? That has been my experience. Experience may not be scientific proof, but experience has value.

What could the efficacious ingredients be? Is it the sugar? Is it the cocoa? Is it the secret formula that the manufacturer has ingeniously spun together? The answer isn't worth worrying about.

Maybe it isn't the ingredients at all. Suppose it's all in our imaginations. What if chocolate is the great placebo and can't really do anything for us? It can't possibly matter. Millions of us "know" chocolate works. And if it works only in our minds, that's sufficient proof for us.

Too much chocolate might lead to severe weight gains, which could leave us depressed. The caffeine in the chocolate might unnerve a few. Like most forms of relief, this one, too, must be watched and controlled. Still, that's no reason to forsake this possibility.

Will it heal us? That might be too strong a statement. Is it a cure? That doesn't sound realistic. But could chocolate help us through the hour? That's a thought we all might want to hold on to.

Break the Routine

It was another day of the same ol' same ol'. Work to do. Schedules to keep. Same town, same office, same lunch hour. Except for this: My wife looked at me and asked, "Would you like to go to a baseball game sometime?"

"Sure!" I replied immediately.

"What team would you like to see play?" she continued.

"The Yankees."

"When are they in Kansas City?" she wondered.

"Right now."

"Let's call and see if we can get tickets," she said eagerly as she rose from the table.

"I doubt it," I concluded.

The next morning we left home at 6:00 A.M., heading southeast to Kansas City. We drove nearly three hundred miles and arrived early for the game. All afternoon we watched batting practice and the game, ate hot dogs and drank pop, cheered and hooted. Home runs soared into the seats and we talked to strangers seated around us.

Fresh air, spontaneity—and did I mention the hot dogs? After the game we drove into Kansas to see our daughter and son-in-law, the fourth state we visited that day. At 1:00 A.M. we drove into our garage and turned off the engine. The next morning we were back at work.

The trip had many ingredients which help one to maintain good mental health. Three of the more obvious are activity, change, and spontaneity. Often the enemies of health are sameness, dullness, and lack of imagination. Some days I feel like my life is so routine, someone should come in every day or two and blow the dust off my head. That's when I know I need a change.

Spontaneity doesn't come easily to many of us. The idea of dropping everything and taking off is frightening when we are used to a carefully measured lifestyle. It's hard enough to say "Let's forget supper and order pizza."

Often it is the inability to loosen up that leads us into serious bouts of sadness.

We can plan activity, but we can't plan spontaneity. Still, we can prepare for it. We prepare by believing spontaneity is a good and acceptable risk, one we need to take to expand our personalities.

Believing that spontaneity is healthy makes it all the more likely to happen. Being impulsive could sometimes be the mature way to behave.

Did I mention those hot dogs?

Take Off the Armor

Ancient knights, decked out in armor, must have been a formidable force in battle. Mounted on giant steeds, they were hard to wound or defeat. Arrows, stones, and even swords bounced off their massive shells.

When a knight arrived home after a hard day battling the pagans and assaulting dragons, he must have been tired. Probably the first thing he did was take off that rigid uniform. But imagine for a moment that he didn't. Suppose he spent the long evening at home dressed in a lobster outfit.

With his armor on, he would be hard to hug. And how could his wife feel his considerable biceps? Or how would his child climb onto his lap? Bouncing on his knee would be like riding in a wagon on a rough road. A baby wouldn't want to cuddle in the crook of his metal arm. He couldn't play ball because he couldn't bend over.

The knight wore armor so he would not be hurt on the battlefield. But the same armor that deflects stones also prevents us from feeling love and tenderness.

Armor keeps us from being injured. Armor also keeps us from feeling warmth.

It's hard to take off the armor. Without armor we are vulnerable. Who knows what might happen if those around us could get to our heart?

Those who want to rise above the pain of depression must remove their armor and take the chance that an arrow might penetrate their heart.

119

They must accept a compliment and not dodge it.

They must admit they can do something well.

They must let go and feel love.

They must agree that they can help others.

They must be open to the spiritual.

They must welcome the potential of who they really are.

Never take the removal of armor lightly. Like molting crabs, we are taking a chance by the very act. Yet, as we drop our protection, many good and wonderful things could happen. It is only by letting our guard down that we open ourselves up enough to allow people to show how much they care.

Arguing With Myself

When you take long walks in the country or stroll along the sidewalks in your neighborhood, do you often argue with yourself? Those discussions are significant, and one would be foolish not to participate.

Something inside—some force, some chemical, some deficiency, some personality quirk—often throws a challenge in my mental path. "Coleman," it says, "you're dumb, you're useless, you get in everyone's way." Exactly where that accusation comes from I have never known, but it's there.

There was a time when I thought there was nothing I could do about this unidentified voice. That is, until I began to exercise more control. If a voice speaks (and I don't mean an audible one), there is a tendency to think it must be the real and only you. If that were so, you would be powerless.

At some moment I decided to talk back. "Stop that!" I told myself. "You must not talk that way." Exercising control is hard, but it can be done.

"I am not useless. I am my grandson's grandfather. I am very useful. My wife loves me dearly. I am a lovable human being.

"If I were no longer here, there would be many gaps that would go wanting. There are children who need attention. Adults who need a good listener. A few people who need an extra dollar now and then. A wife who needs a trustworthy companion and lover."

Arguing with ourselves is an art form and needs to be

121

practiced regularly. The first voice, the negative one, cannot be given sway over our hearts and minds.

Does it get tiresome? Certainly. Arguing with yourself will wear you out. But keeping silent will only dig a deeper hole.

Keep short accounts. Don't let voice number one talk too long. Hush it up quickly. If you listen too long you may weaken and begin to believe the dreadful message.

Stay on top. Talk back. That's what makes those walks so healthful.

Guardian Angels

[His angels] will lift you up in their hands,
so that you will not strike your foot against a stone.
PSALM 91:12

There must be some "extra" characters around who from time to time watch out for us. I find that easy to believe as long as you don't ask me to explain. God has placed a spiritual, nonmaterial world in operation. The only trouble I have is when we try to define it in material, scientific, psychological terms. That's a little like trying to use a baseball bat to explain how football is played.

This is what I have experienced. During some of my darkest periods strange things have happened. Often when I have retreated to my room to sulk and sink into the dungeon of my mind, someone has called. That may not seem odd to those of you who have ten thousand friends, but I don't have anywhere near that many.

The timing often seems too coincidental. Why now? Why you? Someone wants to have coffee, go to a ball game, play Ping-Pong. And I wonder, "Why did you call now? Who sent you? Did you know I was heading for the bottomless dumper?"

Some may think those rare appearances mean nothing. They certainly may be right. Statistical probabilities and all that could probably explain away those situations with barely an effort. But that means we have tried to use a computer to plumb the depths of the spiritual.

The phone calls, the knocks on the door, the convenient interruptions haven't happened every time I've felt lost. Sometimes when they have happened I have even sent the bewildered visitor on his or her way. But inside I have been very grateful that someone, by some means, appeared out of the blue.

We can process that information however we choose. It certainly doesn't all make sense. As for me, I elect to be thankful. Anything that calls me to gratitude is a beautiful gift and I receive it cheerfully.

Swinging Over the Cliff

Not too far from where I lived as a child there was an old tree. Someone had tied a large rope to one of the limbs. Frequently kids would stop and swing on the rope.

The rope would reach far out over a drop-off, which gradually grew quite steep. If you were the careful type, you would swing out only a few feet, where a sudden drop wouldn't hurt so much. The brave or more foolish cast themselves out as far as possible. If they fell, they could break a bone or gash open their skin.

It was one of those "chicken" things. To prove your manhood or your womanhood you might see how far out you were willing to go, and how often you were willing to do it.

Manic depression or bipolar depression is a bit like a rope on a tree. It swings a lot. Sometimes our mood goes way out and is very excited. Next our mood swings back in to become shutdown, careful, even fearful. Those extreme mood swings create a considerable contrast. That contrast is part of why this disorder is so dangerous.

One day you don't need much sleep at all. You think you can do anything. You have the energy of a beehive and you take risks. But before long your rope swings to the other side. Now you can't sleep even though you want to, or you want to sleep all the time. You have barely enough energy to make tea. You're anxious, irritable, and can't believe anything will work out well.

Swinging way up and then way down leaves us worn out and

discouraged. We can't stand the extremes. During the lows we aren't sure how much we want to live.

The good news is that manic depression is highly treatable. Naturally, the sooner it is treated the better. The deeper we get into patterns, the more difficult it may be to turn around.

If your behavior seems strange and lasts very long at all, it is important to check it out. Why take an unreasonable risk by letting your condition grow worse?

Many of us have said, "I wish I had done something about it sooner." With bipolar, sooner is better.

PART FOUR

Sunshine Through the Shadows

Praise be to the Lord,
for he has heard my cry for mercy.

The Lord is my strength and my shield;
my heart trusts in him, and I am helped.

My heart leaps for joy
and I will give thanks to him in song.
PSALM 28:6-7

Laughing at the Donkey

Try to picture life as a vibrant garden. Into that garden occasionally strays a big, floppy-eared, gray donkey. Clumsily he stomps on the beans and kicks at the melons. Oblivious to our presence, he begins eating the carrots, tossing a few here and a few there.

No respectable gardener should be intimidated by the dull-witted buffoon. Go after the awkward beast. Call him names. Throw dirt clods at the intruder. Laugh at him. Drive him away.

Sometimes we take depression too seriously, especially in its early, milder stages. Often we need to laugh at the ugly monsters who try to invade our mental territory.

Imagine depression as a donkey. Give it a name. Call it Duffle. Put a funny hat on it. Tie a cowbell to its tail. Now it will be easier to make fun of when it first sticks its nose inside the garden fence.

"Go away, Duffle! I don't have time for your annoying presence today." Sneak up on him and yell "Boo!" Startle him. Surprise him.

The official term for this is paradoxical intention. Instead of going straight at a problem and handling it with dire seriousness, we run around the end and surprise the demon. Instead of bracing ourselves to resist a problem, we find another way of dealing with it.

If we are afraid of elevators, we learn to make fun of them. If riding in airplanes frightens us, we picture ourselves having a party in the cockpit. Fears are often too important to be dealt with seriously. They need to be treated lightly by the person experiencing them.

One of the first things depression takes from us is our sense of humor. When we lose that defense, our drawbridge is lowered and all manner of barbarians are able to invade the castle of our hearts and minds.

Humor is a powerful tool. Frequently the more serious the situation, the more humor is called for.

Take the test. Do you feel like nothing is funny anymore? Are you losing your sense of the odd and ridiculous? Quickly look down the road. Do you see Duffle the donkey heading for your garden? It's time to hurry out, wave your arms, and make fun of it. Depression can't stand to be laughed at.

What We Do Have

The local optometrist is a fascinating person who takes time to visit and explain everything thoroughly. During my most recent checkup he explained that my eyes had uneven strengths. My left eye gives me a clearer picture than my right eye. As the doctor switched and flipped lenses, the differences between the two were apparent.

I could see out of both eyes, but the focus was certainly not the same.

It's easy for me to imagine that I can look at life through two eyes. From the one eye I can see the many things for which I may be thankful. Out of the other eye I can see a host of problems.

The right eye, where I see mostly the difficulties, is the eye with the poorer focus. The left eye, of thankfulness, lets me see the world more clearly.

Both views are true. Life is sometimes hard and disappointing. My journey is also rich, fulfilling, exciting, and packed with meaning.

Unfortunately, I spend too much time closing my left eye and trying desperately to squint through the right one, which has poorer focus. Seldom do I close the right. Too often I close the left.

The psalmist bubbled over and wrote,

Give thanks to the Lord, for he is good;
his love endures forever.

PSALM 107:1

131

I have to take pills for my health. I hate pills. I can curse them if I want. On the other hand, I can also choose to thank God that they work.

As with many good things in life, thankfulness is a choice. In the midst of the battle we are wise if we choose to be thankful.

Helping Myself

After decades of wrestling with depression, one conclusion has become undeniable. Most of the time I can do something, or a series of things, to help myself. Not only is this true for me, it is also probably true of most of us.

The problem is mustering up the "want to." Hundreds of times I have told myself to simply do three things: grab something to eat, take a short walk, and rent a movie. Those quick steps will almost always bring me back from the edge.

Then why have I so often refused to carry out this simple plan? Because I have known it would work and I haven't wanted it to.

The will to go on was barely there. Optimism and hope, which usually revive the average person, had all but evaporated. Getting energy back is one thing; getting the will back is yet another.

Battling for the will is a fierce struggle involving a number of real but hard-to-identify enemies. Ugly warriors like pride and jealousy take up positions in the mind. Brave soldiers like courage, faith, and love take the field to defend the person they care for. Locked in hand-to-hand combat, each set of forces fights to gain ground.

That very real, and often all too painful, war rages for hours, and sometimes days. The duration of the war and the ultimate victor rest in the decision-making power of the victim. That person must declare his or her will to win.

If the will to win is not seized early, the battle will become entrenched and more difficult to control. The person must decide soon to take the simple solution (whatever that might be), before the struggle gets out of hand.

Today, I fight better because I usually fight early. I know I must handle a problem right away. I must move on now. I must make a call, take a walk, change the setting now. Later the campaign could become much more difficult.

Wisdom often comes from experience. After losing too many struggles, I gained a new resolve. I go at it early. I let courage and faith and love know they can count on me from the very beginning.

Today I know there are ways to help myself.

Do I Deserve Better?

Since I work hard at being a nice guy, I think people should treat me with kindness and deference. After all, my pleasant personality would never upset anyone. Daily I work hard to make sure I step on no toes and ruffle no feathers.

My careful approach doesn't always work. Eventually some snobbish, boorish barbarian is going to treat me terribly. And when someone does, I am shocked. He or she throws sand in my face. Why would anyone want to do that?

After decades of putting on my best face and still occasionally having sand thrown into it, I have reached two conclusions.

First, I'm not as nice a person as I think I am. True, though I'm not a bad guy, despite my best efforts I can be offensive. Let's get real. Good guys mess up more than they think they do.

Because I am a member of this human order I have the potential of turning others off. And so it will always be. It takes a high opinion of oneself to think that one can avoid offending others.

Second, others make mistakes, and that makes them human, too. I can't expect everyone else to treat me fairly. My neighbors and coworkers often have bills to pay, sick children, and a car in the shop. My regular effort to be super-pleasant is no guarantee that others will always respond to me in kind.

This is shocking to people who want to be nice. They think others are obligated to be nice.

The beginning of true humility is to recognize that we cannot control all of our own faults, and that we certainly cannot control the faults of others. Humility can save us from aches, pains, and emotional turmoil.

Being treated unfairly is the lot all of us encounter. To imagine that we might escape only intensifies the agony.

Do I deserve better? No, I do not! When better treatment comes my way, it comes purely as grace. Once I accept that fact, the bumps in life don't hurt quite as much.

Humility turns to gratitude. It makes me thankful for each goodness I receive. Too often it is my pride that traps me and makes me expect "special treatment." Sometimes I get depressed because I am not treated specially. I need to change that.

The Power of Thankfulness

No matter what Erin said to her sister Nancy, Nancy turned it into a negative. If Erin said her sister had a nice car, Nancy would protest that it was not the color she wanted. Erin could talk about Nancy's raise at work; her sister would say it was not enough. This young lady had learned to deflect all hints of thankfulness.

Basic to most forms of depression is a person's ability to reject thankfulness. Nothing is quite good enough. Candy is too sweet. Mountains are too high. Friends are not friendly enough. The sunshine could give you a terrible burn.

Depression is a sure sign that one has soured on life. Though easier said than done, the sufferer needs to begin concentrating on the many joys and gifts this existence has to offer.

The Bible teaches us to come to God with thanksgiving.

Do not be anxious about anything,
but in everything, by prayer and petition,
with thanksgiving,
present your requests to God.

PHILIPPIANS 4:6

What am I thankful for?
The ability to work
A loving other
Long evening walks
Good movies

Terrific grandchildren
Butter brickle ice cream
Friends and coffee
Baseball
Good books
Milk chocolate
David Letterman
Chinese food
Caring children
A dependable car
Fishing in Colorado
Helping others
A good joke
Big Red Football
Planning trips
Sugar-free apple pie
Teaching seminars
Breakfast out
With a list like this it's hard to get down for long.

Weaving Spider Webs

Evidently, spiders do not have to fear their own webs. They weave finely meshed systems to catch prey and furnish food for themselves. Yet, webs are not designed to capture the spiders who make them.

Unfortunately, people aren't nearly as adept when it comes to this craft. We tend to weave webs to protect ourselves, then later we get caught in them.

We devise intricate systems to keep others from getting too close. We don't want to take the risk that someone will get to know us intimately. The idea is to protect ourselves, but ultimately these same webs hold us prisoner. Others cannot get in. We cannot get out.

For instance, if I never give out my phone number, no one can call me. That's my protection. Now turn it around. If I never exchange phone numbers, I have no one to call. Human webs work that way. We get stuck in our own.

Suppose I refuse to go to concerts with anyone else. That's my protection. That way I won't have to go to any concerts that I might not like. Now turn it around. When I find a concert I want to attend, I have no one to call because I have refused the concerts other people liked.

Sometimes I need to get a broom to sweep all the cobwebs away. A few are woven so finely that they are hard to see. Others are caked with dust because they have been around for far too long. One by one I need to clean them out. They are nestled in corners. They hang from the chandelier. They stretch across places I had forgotten.

Then I must resolve to stop weaving them. My obsession with keeping others at a safe distance eventually works to my harm and not to my safety.

Every now and then I make the extra effort to invite people over for the evening. It's risky. There are people I used to invite over who eventually hurt me—bad. For a while I stopped taking risks. Who wants to get hurt? I wove another web.

Today I've knocked many of those webs down. If I do not sweep them away, I cannot reach out to connect. If I do not connect, I am stuck inside my own handiwork.

Erecting doors makes more sense. Doors with large, well-oiled hinges. Doors that swing open freely. Doors that let others in will also let me out.

> *Such is the destiny of all who forget God;*
> *so perishes the hope of the godless.*
> *What he trusts in is fragile;*
> *what he relies on is a spider's web.*
> *He leans on his web, but it gives way;*
> *he clings to it, but it does not hold.*

JOB 8:13-15

The Price of a Nice TV

Say this paragraph out loud: "Honey, I've been thinking about getting help for my depression. It will cost about the same price as a nice television set. It's hard to know which one to spend the money on. Never mind. I've decided to get the TV."

That's a decision people make every day. Most people vote for the television set. They choose the trip to Kansas City, the electric guitar, the dinette set. It happens every day.

Getting counseling is hard. It takes courage and humility to make an appointment and keep it. If we can find an excuse to avoid it, we usually do. The children need sports jackets; dance lessons are expensive; we really want the better caterer at the wedding.

If, however, just one of those items is sacrificed, the children might get a parent who is mentally healthier. There will be fewer moody evenings, anger tantrums, anxiety attacks, and shouting matches. All of that's possible. Yet, in order to get a balanced parent, some item or event will have to be put off.

Given the choice, most of us do not choose to get help. We are consumers. Normally we measure our well-being by what we can purchase and how much we own.

But once in a while someone breaks loose from the pack. He or she stands apart and goes out to get help.

There are people who were once depressed who are now playing with their children. Couples are holding hands and going dancing again. Elderly people are active and have their lives filled with meaning. They broke from the pack and reached out for change.

Though not everyone has found counseling beneficial, the majority of us have. We have discovered everything from personality adjustments to stress management, and the results continue for years.

These are hard decisions to make. Good people have chosen to go for counseling and good people have chosen not to. Those who have gone have taken a positive step when their mental health most needed it.

Choose my instruction instead of silver,
knowledge rather than choice gold,
for wisdom is more precious than rubies,
and nothing you desire can compare with her.

PROVERBS 8:10-11

The Best of Times

There are sunny days when the breeze is to my back and I am sailing steadily across the lake. Sometimes the good times last a day or two, a month or so, or even for several years. That's when I have some idea of where I am going and why I want to get there.

Other days, the boat hardly moves, or it fills with water and sits motionlessly, too swamped to sail on. Those are slow, dark days when the present makes little sense and the future even less. Those days can also stretch out for weeks and months.

What is the difference between the sailing days and the swamped ones? I have found it is *not* my ability to vacation in Colorado or visit the bayous of Louisiana, though trips can certainly help. The more telling difference is whether or not there is presently a sense of meaning and purpose in my life.

Without meaning, Colorado is just another lonely place. Without purpose, Louisiana is simply a getaway.

Life without purpose is a boat without sail or rudder. I need some sense of what I contribute. I don't need to have a high or spectacular calling, such as president of the Red Cross or missionary to Cameroon, honorable as those may be.

The more important question is, "Why do I want to get up tomorrow morning, other than to make a living?"

If there is an elderly person I help watch over, that draws on my spiritual side.

If I spend each Tuesday afternoon painting over graffiti, I reach outside myself.

If I care for my grandchildren one day a week, I know I have purpose.

People who plant flowers at a public park have a reason to get up tomorrow, because they must pull weeds.

Those who write thank-you notes realize that they make a difference in someone else's life. They have a reason or reasons to be here. Life is meaningful because they have a fulfilling connection.

On the contrary, when we get up each morning only to search for ways to make ourselves happy, life becomes a vacuum.

Purpose and meaning are two of the surest cures for daily dejection.

Sleepless Nights

In my younger days, when I was scheduled for a big event the next morning, I would be unable to sleep the night before. At 1:00 A.M. I would still be tossing and turning and mad at myself for not falling asleep.

Now, if I have a big event the following day, I will probably still be awake at midnight. But the big difference is that I am not tossing and I am not mad at myself. I stay awake, accept the fact that sleep won't come easily, and act like an adult.

These are the things I try to keep in mind when I can't sleep.

1. *Stay up.* Don't go to bed until you are sleepy.

2. *Don't stare at the clock.* It's better not to know how much sleep you have missed.

3. *Watch a movie; read a book.* De-reflect.

4. *Eat or drink a little bit.* Don't feel sorry for yourself.

5. *Don't try to go to sleep.* Try to stay awake.

6. *Shorten your night.* Go to bed later, get up earlier.

7. *Think of people to help.* Fill your mind with other people.

8. *Be thankful.* Complaining makes us miserable.

9. *If you are in bed, play the radio.* Music or pleasant chatter will distract you.

10. *Write a letter.* The cleansing process will calm you down.

11. *Sketch pictures of cars and houses.* Artwork can help you think better.

12. *Make a list of places to go.* Imagine yourself in another country.

13. *Pray for God to show you purpose.* You will sleep better if you feel worthwhile.

One of the hardest jobs in the world is to make yourself go to sleep. Fight it. Defy it. Rebel against it like a child does. Soon you will be sleeping like a baby.

Rubber Snakes

E vidently people who have an extreme fear of snakes refuse to look them over. Any mention of the word sends these people scurrying over rocks and through bushes to get as far away as possible. Anything wiggling in the grass or darting a long tongue will put the victim into high gear.

Unfortunately, the sprinter usually takes no time to investigate whether the snake is real or merely a toy. The mesmerizing serpent might be no more than a rubber variety bought at the local novelty store.

Not that I'm critical of people who run from rubber snakes. I have run and hidden from many a phony monster in my life.

Looking back at some of the "rubber snakes" that have chased me off, I now wish I had stayed and checked them over a bit more carefully. Too often I have run from mere shadows, hissing sounds, or slithering noises when I should have stood my ground.

Today I know this much: Most of the snakes in the grass are harmless. They don't bite. They can't squeeze. And they can't swallow anyone.

Too much time is wasted in running. Too often I have ceased perfectly good pursuits in order to find a hoe to defend myself against a viper that didn't exist.

I have found that I feel better when I go toward whatever is after me. I stare into its beady eyes and check out its fangs. I want to see the color of its bands and look at its head to see if it rocks back and forth. And if I hear the distinct rattle of its tail, I will turn around and run like crazy.

It's depressing to be afraid most of the time. We lose our freedom. We sacrifice our dreams on the false altar of anxiety. Too much good energy is wasted worrying that we might be bitten.

The next time I get a nasty letter or a confusing phone call, I need to ask myself if it is a rubber snake. Do I really have reason to be worried, or is it simply a clever illusion?

Calm down. There's no need to panic. It may be a fake adder with no power to do real harm.

In Order to Feel Better

Emily didn't lack for interests. She especially enjoyed an afternoon at the beach, watching the waves break across the shore, digging sand with her toes, and looking for shells. Volunteering for the church preschool on Wednesdays always cheered her up. Emily could name half a dozen activities she normally enjoyed. But recently she hadn't felt like doing any of them.

Someday, Emily told herself, when she felt better, she would rekindle her old interests.

She had convinced herself that when she felt better she would be able to do better. That's why she sat alone, waiting to feel better.

Unfortunately she had the formula backward. No one had explained to this recent college graduate that in order to feel better she must first do better.

If Emily would go to the beach and dig her toes in the sand, she would probably feel better. There are some things we need to do even when we don't feel like it. The decision to carry out these activities could cause us to feel good.

How often do we talk ourselves out of feeling better?

I don't feel like walking.

I don't feel like calling anyone.

I don't feel like volunteering.

I don't feel like painting.

Sometimes we are conscious of what we are doing. We know

that if we show up at the party, we might rise up out of our dullness. Yet, since we aren't ready to give up our despair, we refuse to go. We reject the very activity that might start our healing process.

Health can often be found in participation, personal contacts, creativity, or whatever grabs our attention. When these pockets come to mind, we make decisions to either take a chance and get better or stay where we are and live a little longer in pain. Sometimes a lot longer.

It still happens. Once in a while I sit with the newspaper in my hand, the movie section spread wide open. If I get up and start moving toward the theater, I will come out of the funk I am in. I know that. Now I have to decide if I will get my feet and mind moving or if I will sink back into the chair and stare at the wall. It's my choice.

Driving for Relief

There are two cars in my garage. One has 270,000 miles on it. The other vehicle I still think of as "new." It has only 150,000. If that doesn't seem remarkable, consider the fact that I usually walk to work. My office is three blocks from my house.

At some point in my life I came to look at driving as a healthy exercise. I believe millions of other Americans do, too. The old idea of the Sunday drive has solid therapeutic principles. For an hour or so a person (or a couple) get into a metal capsule, shut out the world, and decompress.

During a long drive we can choose any radio station we want, or no station at all. We can put a hot or cold drink in the cup holder. If it fits our mix we can place a donut or a bagel on the dash for added comfort. Sometimes we bring our significant other along. Sometimes not.

Traveling down the road at sixty miles per hour, we have created a mental oasis. Exactly how healthy the trip might be is in direct relationship to whether we carry a car phone along. A cellular in the trunk for emergencies is one thing, but a cell phone or a pager in our pocket means we are still tethered to the pressure.

Sometimes it is an overload of work and demands that saps our resilience. All of us need some time when we can't be reached. If we have no such time, maybe we need to reshuffle a few responsibilities.

An hour is an excellent break. Half a day is a serious attitude adjustment. An entire day of driving around, stopping for lunch, reading the paper while our mate drives, and listening to tunes can be worth $500 with a psychiatrist.

If it works for you, be sure and do it sooner rather than later. Go, before the ugly monster starts to take over and drag you into the pit. Driving around in total despair can be dangerous. Some of the people who have run stop signs or flipped over in ditches may have been too distracted by gloominess.

I used to feel guilty about driving around. I thought I must be weird to even enjoy it. Why didn't I just stay at home? But today I know four things I didn't know then.

This kind of therapy works for millions of us.

It's a perfectly harmless time out.

If I do it early it keeps me from saying and doing a lot of destructive things.

It's much cheaper than a vacation in the south of France.

If you see me driving on a highway near you with a Nebraska license plate, I may not actually be lost. I may simply be in one of my self-therapy sessions.

Dealing With Hurt

M y feelings are easily hurt. Realizing this should help me get a handle on my problem, though it doesn't always. Reducing my level of hurt will solve many difficult situations that come afterward. If I can keep the hurt to a minimum, I've won half the battle.

Usually, to be hurt is a choice I make. When someone insults me, I make a decision as to what to do with it. When someone says I am dumb, I should be able to "catch" myself and shrug it off. Why do I care if someone else thinks I'm stupid? I have a fairly good perspective on who I am.

That's the way I should handle hurt. But too often I don't. If I don't shrug it off, what is the next best thing?

When an insult or slight bothers me, sometimes I need to voice it: "What you said really hurt me," or "Frankly, I resent what you said." There is no telling what the person may say in reply, but the important thing is that I have addressed the problem. Having a voice can help to clear up the hurt.

When someone hurts me I can either shrug it off or express it. Those are the best avenues to travel.

If I do neither of these, the hurt is likely to turn into anger. Anger becomes a secondary and deeper feeling. Becoming angry will then increase my risk of doing damage either to myself or to a relationship.

If I swallow anger, I am liable to injure myself and my own personality. My feelings could turn to bitterness. If I vent the anger, I could create severe misunderstandings.

There are several ways that all of these mismanaged emotions can be manifested, and most of these, including depression, are harmful.

Understanding the painful trip that could follow, it makes a lot of sense to try to get a grip, and to get that grip early. Managing the hurt is the best hope in the beginning.

"Sticks and stones may break my bones but words will never hurt me" comes close to explaining reality. Most of the time we should become teflon and let insults slide off. Honing this into a fine art would be a major step in maintaining mental health.

A relative cannot cripple us with snide remarks. The words might be cruel, but we are the ones who put ourselves in an emotional wheelchair.

Look at the Benefits

"Frankly, I kind of enjoy my depression," a lady said, to everyone's surprise. "That's the way you have to look at life. If God has allowed me to be depressed, he must have a wonderful reason for it."

She and her ilk talk about the benefits that supposedly come from this debilitating difficulty. They have a bizarre, "look at the bright side" approach to a serious problem.

One person argued that his depression drove him to the edge, and he liked the "heightened" experience that living on the edge gave him. Am I wrong, or isn't that the same excuse drug abusers prattle from time to time?

Granted, there is a thin line between "It's good to get depressed" and "Since I do suffer from depression, I will look for some good in it and make the most of it."

Be certain, mental health is a good thing. The healthier our minds are, the better life will go for us and for those around us. Don't lose sight of this important fact.

It's true, the Bible does say "And we know that in all things God works for the good of those who love him, who have been called according to his purpose" (Rom 8:28).

Be careful as you apply this verse to depression. It does not say everything is good. Neither does it say that God sends everything our way. So don't use this verse to blame God for depression.

Rather, the passage does say this: God can work good out of

everything, especially if we love God and are called according to his purpose.

Depression is not a good gift. We would be better off without it. We really would. However, those who love God may be able to find some good through it.

It is nonsense to think, "Oh, I hope you get depressed. Lying in bed, hating yourself, crying your heart out, entertaining thoughts of suicide, and losing your job have so many excellent benefits. I wish all my relatives could have a heavy dose of this."

Depression is not good. Cancer is not good. Diabetes is not good.

The best answer is: Do what it takes to avoid getting depressed. If you are depressed, look for some help so you can be healthy and even-tempered again.

A Time to Cry

The Bible tells us that Bathsheba was a very beautiful woman. King David saw her taking a bath on the rooftop. Sorely tempted, David arranged to meet her, and before long the married woman was pregnant with his child.

To cover over his sin, the king sent for Uriah, Bathsheba's husband, in hopes he would quickly sleep with his wife. When this ploy failed, David sent Uriah to war. The king also sent a message to General Joab that Uriah was to be sent to the fiercest part of the battle, where he was likely to be killed. And so Bathsheba's husband died.

The Lord sent a message to King David that he would be punished because of this heinous act. Because the king had served God well, his life would be spared but the child would die.

Soon the child became ill. David fasted and lay on the ground all night, begging God to let the child live.

After a week the child died.

The servants were afraid to tell David about the death, but he heard them whispering and demanded to know.

Immediately David got up off the ground. He washed, splashed on some lotion, and put on different clothes. He stopped to worship God and then went home. He ate a fine meal and pulled himself together.

His servants were puzzled. David's grief had seemed genuine enough. He had cried out for the child's life. Why the sudden change?

Thanks for doing that, David. Thanks for showing us that there is a time to fall on our face, and there is a time to get up and go on.

No one seeing the king doubted the sincerity of his pain. But David exercised limitations on his tears.

Too often we let deep grief spill over into all of life. Every river needs a bank. Its waters should be contained within boundaries, if at all possible.

Sometimes depression comes because we forget there is a time to cry and a time to move on, even though it hurts.

Be Happy

When Sara started to depress, before she went too far, she often was able to pull herself off the slippery slope. The college freshman would have a short but frank talk with herself: "I need to do something about this now. What has made me feel this way?"

Once she turned a certain corner, Sara knew she couldn't simply "brighten up." Over the years she had learned to take action early, knowing that otherwise it might be days or even weeks before she could get back on top.

If we are reasonably healthy, for most of us our condition is fairly manageable. In a sense our mental state sometimes comes to a fork in the road. We need to recognize that if we don't handle what is bothering us, our direction will go dangerously downhill.

How often have we said to ourselves, "If I sit here and sulk I will become angry"? That means we still have considerable control over the situation and need to get moving. If we leave ourselves to the forces of mental gravity, we're taking a terrible risk.

Sometimes I've simply said to myself, "Be happy" and then pursued whatever it took to follow my chosen path.

Get walking. Go driving. Clean out the garage. Mow the lawn. Start calling. Do something while you still can. It works.

To "be happy" is much more difficult—not impossible, but much more difficult—after I pass a certain mile marker. Later it may take major excavation to dig myself out of miserable mire.

Two truths seem self-evident. First, sometimes I am quite capable of reversing a day's dark beginning. Second, sometimes I am nearly helpless to pick myself up. I am also convinced that no one else can tell us which day we can and which day we cannot stabilize our mental outlook all by ourselves.

We have a wide arsenal at our disposal. We might be able to fight depression with good counseling, by getting rid of a bad habit, by being with friends, by faith, by gardening, or sometimes with medication. Sometimes a big part of these weapons is the decision to "be happy."

Some days we need to give it a try. A direct choice will save us a great deal of later grief.

Become My Own Friend

Today I need to stand beside me. I need to remind myself that I'm worth being around. I need to get close, even intimate, instead of running away from who I am.

Who I am sometimes frightens me. I think I must be some sort of monster: an unpleasant person, irritating, boring, a menacing sort.

I could always sense that others didn't care to be around me. Was it the dirty clothes, the odd-sized shoes, the look of uncertainty and fear? Early on you learn. You sense how different you must be. And yet at first you can't begin to understand how you can be different.

When you hit twenty, sail past thirty, and climb the last rungs on the ladder to forty, you have a sense that nothing has changed. The clothes are clean and your well-polished shoes match. But still you have the sense that people don't care to be around you.

Sometimes you try to stand straight and unmovable, like a rock. Sometimes you bend like a palm tree, pliable, cheerful, breezy—whatever the occasion might demand.

Yet either way you soon drift back into who you really are. You can pretend for only so long. Soon you again wonder why others do not feel at ease with you.

Today I need to stand beside me. I need to look at myself and smile. I need to give myself the kind of released, accepting look that says I enjoy being with you.

I need to open up and accept my own friendship. I need to say "I'm OK." I need to know someone thinks I'm worth knowing. And that someone has to be me. Then I will be able to fully accept and fully enjoy friends who want to be with me. But first I have to reach my arms around myself and tell myself I'm glad I'm me.

A Letter to Depression

Dear Depression,

Are you still around? Like an aging, overweight boxer you have stayed far past your prime. You don't have the same punch you used to have. Once in a while you get in a sharp jab, but it's nothing like the power you carried in the old days. You are a caricature of your old self.

Sorry, but you're almost comical. I can see you coming, breathing hard, legs of lead. Each swing you take is cumbersome and labored. If I'm half alert I can dip or dodge before you land a blow.

In the old days I couldn't get out of the way, but today I'm quite a bit sharper and you are definitely slower.

When I see you coming I grin a little, pull myself up out of the chair, and get moving. Off to see a friend for coffee, I won't even be around by the time you get within twenty feet. I have things to do and places to go. I have dreams to see come true. You won't find me in bed, sulking. Life's too exciting.

Look at yourself. Some terrible depression you are. More a clown than a challenger. And to believe that I once thought I was no match for the likes of you.

The only way you can get me these days is if I get out of shape. If my spirits sag, my mind droops, or my soul gets stuffy, then you might, that is *might*, hit me when I'm sluggish. But I try to keep sharp so you don't have a chance.

Honestly, I still have a smidgen of respect for you, but only that. You hold no terror unless I allow you to. You are weak on your own.

Take off your fighter's gloves and put on your clown nose. Trade in your boxing shorts for baggy pants and floppy shoes. You simply aren't what you used to be around here.

Disrespectfully yours.

Is That All There Is?

There is a song with this title about a father who took his little girl to the circus. After looking at all three rings, she turned to her father and asked, "Is that all there is?" After each part of her life she would wonder the same thing.

One of my better thoughts is that this is not all there is. My conversion helped me tremendously in this regard. I look at life with a definite tilt because I believe there is another life to follow this one.

Presently my life is good. Yet there are days when it absolutely stinks. Those days that are dull, slow, and even abrasive are much easier to handle because I believe that this is not all there is. I don't have to make every day count. I don't have to panic because this day won't have enough excitement in it. When these days are over, there is another life on the other side.

I do want to make my life worthwhile. I want it to have meaning and purpose. But every hour? It's fun to while away sixty minutes here and ninety minutes there.

This go-around doesn't have to be perfect. I'd like for it to be a good journey, but I can afford to toss a few days here and there into the wind.

That thought helps me recover after being down. Maybe I went into the dumper and didn't talk to anyone all weekend. Maybe I went to work in zombie fashion, barely placing one foot in front of the other. When I do come out of the pits I don't have to feel so guilty about it.

This life is not all there is. In the next life I'm going to do better. I don't know how and I don't know why, but I will. In the next life I won't have my present chemistry. My background will be different. I'll have a terrific set of coping skills. And, of course, I won't have to cope with the same problems I face here.

That frees me up. My days are more like panning for gold. One day is a stone. The next day medium grade. The third day is pure gold. I get more gold than I realize.

When I get discouraged I don't have to dump the entire pan into the stream. There are some stones, a few medium grade, and a good number of gold nuggets.

If every day has to be gold, I will feel like a failure in this life. That's unnecessarily gloomy.

I can't promise myself that every day will be great. But I'm going to find enough good ones to make the trip worthwhile. And when all else fails, I'm going to think about the good times, and remind myself that heaven's going to be even better.

Always be full of joy in the Lord; I say it again, rejoice! Let everyone see that you are unselfish and considerate in all you do.

Remember that the Lord is coming soon.

Don't worry about anything; instead, pray about every-thing; tell God your needs, and don't forget to thank him for his answers.

If you do this, you will experience God's peace, which is far more wonderful than the human mind can understand. His peace will keep your thoughts and your hearts quiet and at rest as you trust in Christ Jesus.

PHILIPPIANS 4:4-7, LB

PART FIVE

Helping You Help Me
Find the Sunshine

Save me, O God,
for the waters have come up to my neck.

I sink in the miry depths,
where there is no foothold.

I have come into the deep waters;
the floods engulf me.

I am worn out calling for help;
my throat is parched.

My eyes fail,
looking for my God.
PSALM 69:1-3

Easy Answers

One of the Kennedys is credited with saying, "To every complicated problem there is a simple solution. And it is always the wrong one."

We all want easy answers. That's why medication is so popular right now. We want a magic pill. A young man was addicted to drugs and was in the process of wrecking his life. When one of his relatives heard about the addiction, he replied, plain as toast, "Tell him to stop using."

Why hadn't someone thought of that? Tell overweight people to eat less. Hide an alcoholic's bottle. Tell a smoker to eat candy. Challenge people who are afraid, "Don't fear." Easy answers sound good, but only because we don't want to take the time to get to know people and their problems.

Mental health problems are often complex. People who struggle with depression do not have an easy road to travel, and being told to "go that way" isn't going to cure them. The suggestions in this book are not intended to be "quick fixes." Often what works well for Person A does not work at all for Person B.

When it comes to mental illness, healing often takes place through a process of trial and error. Frequently the things that helped us five years ago are totally ineffective today. Consequently, we are forced to look around and discover a few more devices, remedies, and distractions.

The support of friends and family makes a big difference, of course. We learn to be wary of well-meaning "encouragers" who shrug us off with flippant prescriptions:

"You need to get out more."

"Have you tried cranberry juice?"

"Don't you know people don't like to be around people who are depressed?"

"Put one finger on each side of your mouth and push a smile back."

Easy answers like these don't help. More often, they compound the problem.

If you know someone who struggles with depression, this section is for you. There may be a way for you to help that person experiment with the remedies that seem to work for him or her. You may be able to refer that person to a good counselor, not one with a two-step program. Someone who is a good listener and who is not afraid to check out the wound with the one who is depressed.

Most of all, you can pray. Pray for the depressed person, that the way will become bright again, and the reasons for the darkness revealed. Pray for yourself, too, for greater compassion and wisdom in knowing how to help.

Depression is often many-faceted. Help might come from four or five directions. Those who are persistent in checking out those directions may make the best progress.

Let all who take refuge in you be glad;
let them ever sing for joy.
Spread your protection over them,
that those who love your name may rejoice in you.

PSALM 5:11

When I'm Afraid to Let It Go

We are amused when well-meaning folks tell us to "get over it." Apparently they think depression is like watching television. All we have to do is turn off the blasted thing. As one woman said of a young man who was an alcoholic, "Why doesn't he just stop drinking?"

The answer is rather easy. If we stop being depressed, where will we go? An animal hates to be run out of the bushes if it will immediately be exposed and become easy prey for hunters, vultures, or other predators.

Too many relatives, friends, and neighbors take sticks and try to chase us out of bushes. "Just get moving," they say, or "Stop acting like that," in an attempt to change us. Their philosophy is similar to the old idea, "Throw the child in the river and he will learn to swim."

Those who would prod and force us to leave the cave of depression must first help us find a place to go. They dare not tell us to run free among the lions and see if we get eaten.

If we are expected to leave Port A, give us some idea of what Port B will be like. Then listen carefully if we tell you Port C or even Port D sound more suitable. Never impose your port on another person. Provide a map and point to five or six ports, then be available to answer questions.

Not everyone is happy to leave the pier, even if it is on fire. Some may choose to fight the fire rather than jump into the sea, if they feel they will certainly drown.

Friends who want to help will join the depressed person and patiently help that person find a safe place. The meaningful words here are *join, patiently,* and *safe.*

A depressed person might be saying to him- or herself, "Dull, dank depression is working for me." As miserable and boring as it may be, those of us who are depressed believe this enables us to survive. Don't tell us to let go unless you first help us find another place to go.

How Does It Feel?

Allow me to explain how depression feels for me. It won't match everyone's experience. There are different depths and different directions to depression. I know only how I felt, and how I still feel occasionally.

Depression for me is an attempt to stop feeling. And yet it goes beyond that. Feelings of emptiness, worthlessness, and uselessness are quite acceptable at the time. Apparently I head for a pocket of feelings where I will not be disturbed by hope, light, or the future.

That's why I don't want to eat. Food is a vote to live. When I am down I don't want to acknowledge any desire to go on. After all, going on is painful, dark, and hopeless. Even in my darkest moments I can think it through, if ever so poorly. My vote has already been cast that life as I know it should end. Eating puts me at odds with my own feelings.

The minute I eat something I know the depression has been broken. Energy will soon be released in my body and mind. The downward cycle has been broken.

Being around people has the same effect on me. I must avoid everyone in order to maintain my dank despair. If I say something or get into a conversation, the spell is at least half broken. Talking is for me the denial of depression. If I am willing to engage in simple talk, I know life has meaning and should continue.

Total isolation robs life of purpose and context for most of us. People furnish the human connection. If we acknowledge people, they can give worth to our existence.

The presence of one person who might care whether I exist or not could draw me back into the circle of the truly living. I know that. And it scares me.

Therefore my first need, if I am to be deeply depressed, is a lair where I can avoid human contact. When a person shows up I must immediately wrestle with the decision: Do I want to come out of this now or not?

Should the person demand that I come out of it immediately, I simply burrow in deeper. However, if that person lets me know he or she is available when I want to come out, I am far more likely to pull myself together.

Sometimes my wife leaves some tea and cookies by the door. Sometimes a note. Other times she will go to bed and let me stay downstairs and begin to throw off the shell gradually.

It used to happen a lot. It still happens now and then. But through it all she stays around and shows how much she cares.

Who Really Knows?

I know how you feel. I felt terrible when the stock market dropped a few years ago." This person meant to be helpful, but she really didn't have a clue. She had been disappointed. She had experienced the blues. Yet, fortunately for her, she had no real idea of what depression can be like.

Serious depression is like a pall that settles over us. More than merely affected by depression, we are actually draped with it. The word *pall* comes from the word *appallen*, which means to become pale. For a while our soul becomes pale and we lose interest in life and its many facets.

The person who strikes out in a ball game and then doesn't feel like eating has only tinkered with depression. At ten o'clock tonight he will eat a dish of Rocky Road ice cream and bounce back. He doesn't understand the person whose soul has turned ashen.

Only the truly patient person takes time to hear how we feel. Few have time. The sad part is that many try to speed up the process by saying, "I know just how you feel."

You cheapen our feelings by blurting out, "I know ..."

Even the poor sufferer does not really know precisely how he or she feels.

If you choose to help, you must be willing to listen. Listening is hard work. Never enter into it lightly. Hear us out. Encourage us to talk more. Listen in order to understand. If you don't understand, ask us to explain it again. Listen for feelings and not merely for words. What do we mean by what we say? Good listening is heavy lifting. No wonder most people don't choose to participate.

All too often people listen only so they can interrupt by telling a story they have just remembered. They are less interested in our stories and more interested in theirs.

"I know. I know." Those are not the words of a truly understanding helper. They are instant responses to deep-seated grief, loss, pain, and despair.

Like fog, a pall is not easily lifted from an individual's soul. But it happens. Kind, patient listeners are the ones who allow it to happen.

Be Sure and Ask

Tony knew every meaningless cliché about depression. When his wife went to her room and refused to come out, he decided to go in and tell her everything he knew.

"Some people use depression as a way of getting attention," he told her with an air of authority. Then Tony stared at his wife so she would realize that he was fully aware of the game she was playing. He expected her eyes to light up with an admission that this was her ploy.

Tony thought he possessed special insight into the feelings of others.

"Come on, honey," he tried again. "If you pull out of this we can go out to dinner."

He grinned to show what a pleasant, cheerful human being he was. He thought, "How could anyone stay down with a natural charmer like me around?"

Tony was riding on good intentions but little else. Instead of tearing down walls, he was actually building them higher. He could have saved everyone a shipload of grief if he had known a few basic pointers.

Unfortunately, Tony acted as if depression is depression is depression. "What's the big deal?" he seemed to assume. "If you've seen one depression, you've seen them all."

He failed to listen and learn from his wife. Tony's failure to listen only clogged up the communication lines.

He pushed her to speak up right then. Because he did that,

she sealed her lips for the time being. He failed to be a caring husband who was available when she wanted to talk.

Tony implied that his wife wasn't really sick but rather playing games. Calling her motives into question let her know that he not only didn't trust her, but even trivialized her condition.

Why would she want to talk to him? He had done little more than belittle and insult her feelings.

If we want to know how people feel, the only dependable way is to ask them. To tell people how they feel stops us from gaining any real knowledge of their pain. How can we hope to join a person in his or her healing if we don't even have the patience to let that person speak?

Don't Label Me

We enjoy labeling people. It's simple. It's quick. It eliminates the hard work of getting to know someone. It also makes us feel smart because we think we can wrap a person with one package and place a name on it, similar to the packaging in a department store.

If you don't have the time or the interest to get to know me, please don't stick a label on me. Don't mark me "acute depressive," or "passive aggressive," or that old standby "co-dependent." For the same reasons, I resist being called Republican or Democrat, liberal or conservative.

All my life I have silently screamed that I am a person and not a category. To simply call me a name is to diminish me as an individual and deny my self-worth.

To say that I sometimes suffer from depression is only a description of some of my behavior. It is nowhere close to understanding who I am.

There was a time when doctors would refer to "the gallstone in room 123." They now work hard to see cases as people. Never say I am obsessive-compulsive or an existential vacuum. I may have behavior like that, but I am not that.

I am a person. I dare you to get to know me.

Not only is it insensitive and superficial to label me, but the practice is also self-fulfilling. If someone tells me I am manic depressive and I believe that person, I will begin to live out the symptoms. By evening I will be having roller-coaster highs and lows. After all, isn't that what I am supposed to do?

Who hasn't been in a conversation where you were asked where you grew up, where you went to school, and what jobs you have had? In a few minutes the interviewer may conclude you are a southerner with a liberal education who identifies with conservative causes. In fact, the opposite may be true. But then, why take time to get to know someone?

Much emphasis is placed on diagnoses, both on the professional level and in self-help books. Some children even want to go to a therapist and get a label. Like designer clothes, they want the "in" diagnosis.

My life is too personal to fall neatly into someone's category. If you want to know me, please hear me out.

Please Tell Me This

We are all individuals and we each react differently. The following are a few statements that I have found helpful when I am heading into depression.

- *"If you want to go to a movie, go out to eat, or take a walk, I'll be available."* This offers a selection from which I can choose.

- *"I'll be downstairs if I can help."* This is good proximity but not in my face.

- *"Remember, I love you."* This is a great tent peg in a storm.

- *"Is there something you want to tell someone?"* A listener is within range.

- *"I've had similar experiences, but none just like yours."* That shows respect for my individuality.

- *"You seem to be in a great deal of pain."* This acknowledges that my hurt is real.

- *"Would you like some tea or toast?"* That's a crack in the door, and I might take it.

- *"I'll just place the newspaper outside your door."* You have made contact with a subtle alternative.

Sometimes you can help without saying a single word. Here are some things my wife has done that have helped me get out of the dumper.

- *Leave a note someplace.* Place a short, positive note on the table or under the door.

- *Touch me as you leave.* Brief physical contact calms me down.

Don't Tell Me That

When I'm down and staring at the floor, I know you want to be helpful. Though you are eager to pull me up, there are certain things I wish you would not say. They only drive me down.

- *Don't tell me you know how I feel.* Ask me if you want to, but don't assume you know.

- *Don't tell me what to do.* Orders or directions scare me.

- *Don't belittle me or my feelings.* "This will all blow over" is too simplistic.

- *Don't become impatient.* "Well, after another hour you need to snap out of this."

- *Keep any clichés to yourself.* "Life isn't fair." "We all get down sometimes," and so on.

- *"This is a bad example to others."* This suggests I can't be a person.

- *Don't call this a phase.* "Someday you'll look back at this and laugh."

- *"It's all in your head."* So what does that prove?

- *"Are you happy with your weight?"* A put-down on top of my own put-downs.

- *"The choice to be depressed is up to you."* Sometimes, but only sometimes.

- *"Giving up is for cowards."* The word *coward* is highly inflammatory and useless.

- *"My aunt was depressed and she killed herself."* Thanks for the encouragement.

> *An anxious heart weighs a man down,*
> *but a kind word cheers him up.*
>
> PROVERBS 12:25

Snap Out of It

High on the list of dumb things to say to a depressed person is, "Why don't you snap out of it?" The person who says it shows a severe lack of understanding and a lack of compassion.

It's like telling someone with the flu, "Why don't you snap out of it?" Or try telling a person who is $1,000 overdue at the bank, "Why don't you snap out of it?" The statement assumes that the individual is in total control of the situation.

It would be nice if people were always capable of snapping out of their problems, but when it comes to depression it isn't that easy. Especially if someone else tells you to.

The command itself tells us quite a bit about the person barking orders. First, this person fails to comprehend the nature of the beast. He or she doesn't understand how depression operates. Two, the outsider has grown impatient and does not care to stand by and wait for the sufferer to get better. "I want you to be healed and I want you to heal now."

This is the irony of it all. When a person begins to sink into the dark lake, there is some possibility that he or she can snap out of it. This person might tell himself, "I don't want to go there, I will turn it around." But when another person demands that he or she snap out of it, a depressed person becomes like a turtle that pulls inside its shell and drops further into the mud.

A depressed person responds by thinking: "They think this is simple; they believe depression is no big deal; if I turn around

185

now they will believe I was faking." He or she pushes further down. The window of opportunity passes by and depression will probably last a bit longer now.

Back off. Give the sufferer some breathing room. Let this person expand and retract his or her lungs for a while. If we show respect for the depressed person's problems, the very dignity of it all may give this person the freedom to work through the problems and come out of his or her shell when ready.

Depression is real. It isn't a cloud of smoke. We can't just brush it away. Depression is not an illusion that afflicts the weak. Some of the strongest people fall victim to its curse.

Friends who want to help friends must first accept their illnesses for what they are.

CONCLUSION

How to Cope When Someone You Love Is Depressed

by Pat Coleman

One beautiful summer afternoon Bill and I were at Kaufmann Stadium, enjoying a Kansas City Royals base-ball game. Seated next to Bill was a single father with his two-year-old and five-year-old sons. The tikes were dressed in blue team shirts and wore Royals baseball caps. Bill and the father talked about the stats of various players and how the pitching game was going.

Meanwhile the dad kept a close eye on the two-year-old, who was constantly squirming, wiggling, climbing, pushing, laughing, or crying. When the boy took a sip of ice cold lemonade, the tanginess caused him to spit it out, sending a spray on the unsuspecting spectator seated in front of him. The dad apologized and the spectator laughed it off. Later the little fellow was eating a slushie and accidently dumped it down the shirt of the spectator. I stifled outbursts of laughter at this entertainment.

As we were driving home that evening, it occurred to me that the wonderful little boy was being a perfect two-year-old. He was behaving exactly as a two-year-old should have.

Someone who is depressed cannot be expected to behave as other than he is. He is hurting. He is feeling useless. He is feeling hopeless. He is probably unable to be kind or thoughtful or cheerful or optimistic or strong or any other attribute that you are looking for.

You must find strength within yourself not to expect your loved one to be other than he is. Believe he wants to behave differently than he is behaving at the time. Believe he will come back. Believe his love for you is not diminished. He probably does not like himself at the time and he cannot find the wherewithal to behave as he really wants to. You have to accept him as he is until he is able to move out of the depression.

You must show him that you love him very much. You are there for him, and will still be here as long as he needs you. Maybe you will be able to say it with words. But if he will not hear you, try to show your love. Sometimes that may mean sitting with him; sometimes it may mean leaving him alone. There is no way of knowing exactly what he will accept at the time. Watch and listen.

As much as possible, maintain your normal schedule. If you usually make meals at certain times, follow that same schedule. If you normally go for walks in the evening, invite him even if you think he'll refuse.

Help him in his obligations if you can, but don't try to cover for him. If he misses an appointment, you must be straightforward and not lie to the one he breaks faith with.

It will be painful when your loved one is in depression, just as it is painful when a family member must fight cancer, heart trouble, or any disease. Your job is to be supportive and gracious and generous.

Your loved one may seem like a porcupine with its bristles extended. He may seem to push you away, he may glare at you, he may appear to be blaming you for his situation. Don't push into his territory until you're invited.

The feeling of isolation at those times is overwhelming for me. I am grateful for a special friend who listens when I say "I am hurting." Rather than stuff the hurt inside, I survive much better when I am candid about my fears and pain with my friend. Remember, it's a two-way street. My friend is human and has hurts, and because I am open with her, she feels free to confide in me when she needs a listening ear.

If you did something wrong and feel you caused him to go into depression, here are two suggestions: (1) apologize or explain what happened if possible, and (2) realize there are other ways to handle disagreements, and depression is not a good choice. He is the one who chose depression.

Try to be extra alert and positive during periods of depression. Don't bring up the tax bill or broken equipment. Your loved one has all he can handle at the moment. Handle the household by yourself as best you can. Sometimes things won't get taken care of in the way you had hoped. Your house doesn't have to be perfect.

Sometimes I have cried because I loved Bill so much and he was hurting so deeply and I couldn't help him, and I was being pushed away. But at those times we realize how much we love each other, our hearts are softened, and somehow we regain strength to rise up to wholeness.

I'm glad I stuck around through the bouts of depression.

Many waters cannot quench love,
neither can the floods drown it.

Song of Solomon 8:7, kjv

Helps for Preventing Depression

These are some secrets we have learned to help ward off the monster, depression:

- LISTEN, LISTEN, LISTEN. When your spouse wants to talk, aim to be approachable and flexible. If possible, stop what you're doing in order to listen, hear, and ask questions.
- Honesty is essential. Trust each other.
- Keep your priorities straight. Your spouse is your first priority.
- Talk things through. If you do or say something for which you need to apologize, do it right away.
- When your spouse messes up, try to be gentle. Treat him as you wish to be treated.
- Try to be generous with praise for all your spouse does well: being a responsible, dependable, thoughtful, fun husband; being a good grandfather; handling his business well. On my desk I keep a picture of Bill as a three-year-old to remember that he may need an extra amount of praise and appreciation because he was not nurtured as a boy.
- Thank your spouse for the ways he has enriched your lives together. Be specific.
- Once a week have a business lunch. Whatever needs to be handled (including family and home) can be put into the file to be discussed and decided upon at that meeting. This avoids having to hash out items of small importance on a day-to-day basis.

Here are some other things I have found helpful in coping with my husband's depression. Depending on your circumstances, you might find these helpful, too.

- On Friday evenings we plan some activity or get together with friends. Sitting home on Friday evenings is a downer for us.
- We plan a trip once every season. At this stage of our lives, the anticipation plus time away is great for us.
- We prepare ourselves carefully when houseguests are coming. We are careful not to become overtired and to take time away for just the two of us as needed—whether going out for a movie or going to bed early one evening.
- A fire in the fireplace is great for relaxing, particularly in times of stress.
- We never skip meals and we have snacks each evening.
- I keep the house orderly—not perfect, but orderly—and I do the laundry each Tuesday.
- I have removed some cutting words from my vocabulary. "You never take me out to eat" is now "I'd love to have dinner out with you this weekend."
- I try to remember that I am loony, too. We are human. That's OK. Life is full of problems to solve.
- I pray for both of us. Our conversion experiences are similar and we share like faith and find comfort in Scripture.